THE FILIPINOS IN AMERICA

THE FILIPINOS
IN AMERICA

by Alfredo N. Munoz

Library of Congress Catalog Card Number 77-186813

Manufactured in the United States of America
Mountainview Publishers, Incorporated
Los Angeles

INTRODUCTION

In compiling this book I did the expected and the possible. I "waylaid" people in the streets, button-holed them in restaurants, and abused their hospitality at home. I joined dozens of Filipino organizations, one of which I did join because of a remark, said in jest but effective nonetheless, that the reason I was always around was because of the free meal I got for being a guest.

I stood sponsor to weddings and baptismals. I attended innumerable affairs. I got myself invited to religious conferences, even having to represent certain denominations outside my faith. I drove through 100 miles of fog in the freeway to hear a Philippine bishop talk for three hours about American missionaries in the country, and conversely, about Philippine missionaries in the U.S. today. I lost good money on horses and cockfights and mah-jongg because of *pakikisama* (deep sense of camaraderie).

Through three years, I had the good fortune of running into hundreds of people, now friends (?) of mine. From them I got the kind of assistance I needed. For how was I to know, for instance, that a Filipino community existed in Hawaii as early as 1870 . . . that the first football hero produced by the Pinoys in America is not Roman Gabriel but Richard Dagampat . . . that Carlos Bulosan, of *New Yorker* magazine fame, had to get himself drunk in the manner of Edgar Allen Poe before attempting a story, essay or poem? — public libraries, as it were, hardly yielding anything of consequence on the subject.

Relatives, provincemates (from Albay) and former students of mine in the Philippines were also most anxious to help, and were helpful. This meant, for me, long distance calls from my home base in Los Angeles, and long extended trips to Hawaii, San Francisco, San Jose, San Diego, Seattle, Las Vegas, Chicago and New York. The result is this book which I hope will not only be diverting but informative and perspective-setting as well.

— A. N. M.

Los Angeles, California, U.S.A.

CONTENTS

ACKNOWLEDGMENT

This book is a community effort more than a personal one. Many contributed towards its completion. Among those immediately coming to mind are: Isagani Pastor, Romy Madrigal, Victor Zapanta, Florencio Dumapias, Manny Mationg, Lourdes Lardizabal, the Bellezas (Ramon, Ruperta, Teddy and Allen), Domingo Reyes, Amor Manligas, Marcos Mata, Nerio and Zeny Katigbak, Julio Villaflor, Ignacio Amador, Roy Berces, the Buenaflors (Bernie and Madge), Consul Ruperto Baliao and Al Evans.

Gratitude is likewise extended to Royal Morales, Dr. Antonio Saqueton, Rod Estrada, Pete Lagusay, Almino Ancelmo, Gene Chin, Jocelyn Geaga, Jean Docena, Dr. Mike Geronimo, Paul Pauler and Richard Dionzon for suggestions given, remarks said or ideas expressed knowingly or unknowingly; and to Consul General Trinidad Alconcel of Hawaii, Consul General Jose Toribio, Jr. of Seattle, Consul General G. Bisnar of Vancouver, Consul General Pacifico Evangelista of Los Angeles, former Congressman Barney Menor of Hawaii, Cedar Pastor, Professor Manuel S. Rustia, Ambassador Alejandro Holigores and Senator Jovito Salonga for stimulating conversations on the subject.

The irrepressible hospitality of Consul General Carlos Faustino of San Francisco, and that of Nelly Smith-Pamatmat of Seattle, Rick Medina and A. B. Sevilla of Maui, Lourdes V. Palacio of Vancouver, Gerardo Casuga of Orange Cove, Fr. Tim Quintero of Honolulu, Divina Valencia Vuich and Nena Amaquin of San Diego, Carmen G. Tomek of Stockton was crucial to this book; so was the enthusiasm shown by the Batongmalaques (Hermie and Dr. Jenny), Connie Osberg, Pat Martin, Adelaide Galpo, Isabel Smith, Mary Balinsat, Janet Esco, Peachy Belit, Dolores Pulido, Annie Batnag, Maura Olano, Danny San Juan, Greg and Mike Mariano, Luz and Ador Paner, Dolly Apolinar, Lauro Natividad, Pat Ugalde, Ferdie Trinidad, Isabel Trenholme and Eriberto Santa Ana.

A great amount of indebtedness is acknowledged to Rudy Buyagawen and all the Buyagawens, Dagans and Quintoses for providing me fresh materials to work on; to Marcial Pamintuan for the chapter on navy men; to Antonio Abagon, Calvin Chao, Vic Lingan and Marcial Reyes for legal guidance; to Alfonso Sauz for the lowdown on Guamenian Filipinos and to Theodore Dichirico, Marcy Ines, Felicidad Muzar, Elizabeth Romack, Pastor D. Mondok, Dick Padrone, Jimmy Smith, Nony Capellan and Ralph Brambles for obliging more than willingly to my requests.

There were other things, too: Joseph Sureck's offer to assist in matters regarding immigration; Dick Quiep's invaluable tips; Bart Moore's poetic insights. Dr. Jose L. Romero's prescription for long life, based on nightly sex, while giving me a chuckle, has left me a doubtful frame of mind.

All through three years (1969-1971), I was fortunate to have had associations with Bonnie and Marie Glory, Paul Reyes, Josephine Brown, Ivy Villalino, Nick and Liza Segundo, Thelma Gunia, Rowley and Prudy Fischer, Margaret Lavelle, Fr. Franklin Ruetz, Ray St. Cyr, Margie Ells, Salvador San Agustin, Zosimo Majuelo, Johnny Carandang, Frank Rabena, Ernie Limcaco, Ralph Duarte, Kenneth Hope, Ron Jacobus, Dick Hermosura, Elmer Escuadro, Joe and Jean Abella, Ray Verdugo, Mario Domino, Albert Allen, Maring and Dulce Geaga, Dr. Roland Navarro, Vidal Vitor, Harry Taylor, Romeo Salumbides, Norman Girard, Tony Reyes, Fe Cunanan and the Krisdorfers.

Industrialist Felix K. Lirag was instrumental in affording me a chance to check and double-check my sources. Jaime Licuanan proved to be a 24-carat friend: he lent me his best overcoat for my trips to Canada and the East, even if he had as much use for the same in the Carolinas. Art Duchane did all the illustrations from memory. Joseph L. Lardizabal undertook the nitty-gritty part of appending, indexing,typing and retyping of names and organizations.

In a larger sense, therefore, the credit goes to all the persons mentioned here and to the hundreds and hundreds contacted and interviewed for the purpose. All I did was record and interpret feelings, ideas and sentiments. I would hasten to add, however, that I, alone, am responsible for all the faults and limitations of this compilation.

To my wife
FLORENCE
and my son
ROCKY
who in many ways
helped nourish this book to life

By the same author

OUTSTANDING FILIPINOS: THEIR FIRST JOBS

PART ONE

A PLACE IN A NEW WORLD

CHAPTER I

INSOMNIACS NO MORE

The Filipino image in America today is no longer a little brown man working his way through a mountain of dishes, nor a weary-eyed fruit picker teetering between insomnia and vagrancy. He is now a well-heeled doctor, a bank clerk and for the most part a charming lady in white — responsive and responsible, hard-working, even-tempered, sufficiently knowledgeable, although a bit inadequate in subtleties. The doctor inspires confidence in his patients, the bank employee is reasonably held in trust, the nurse seems to fill her part well enough.

The new image emerged with the influx of professionals who came as exchange students, then as immigrants after the Second World War. Those who could not come as such came anyway under subterfuge, managing to stay for long periods of time, even gaining permanent residency, to the chagrin of immigration authorities. Customs officials in Honolulu, Anchorage, Seattle, San Francisco and Los Angeles are said to lose their sense of humor immediately upon having to put up with tourists and students, or for that matter, anybody bearing Philippine passport.

But outside this kink, which subjectively, is more a tribute than an offense to the host country, the new breed of Filipinos are welcome anywhere in America. They are liked for what they are—for what they can do—and not because of some glorious considerations. To the average American ties of friendship and history or special relations in trade and the military, while great, hardly carry any weight in the matter of employment.

The Filipino seeking the gleam must therefore know the hard-core rules at survival in America. What that means is that he must have the hardware—the skill, the imagination, the aptitude, the hardiness, the exuberance, the forbearance, the money-lust. Which qualities are not hard to find in a native whether hailing from Magsingal, Ilocos Sur; Arayat, Pampanga; Libon, Albay; Dulag, Leyte or Malaybalay, Bukidnon. And which are not wanting in the post-war immigrant whose senses have been honed to razor readiness, and who before coming makes it a point to pick up other trades like automotive and carpentry (for the male doctor), hair-styling, dress-making and dry-cleaning (for the nurse), just in case.

Like those preceding them, immigrants upwards 1945 are predominantly Ilocanos. They come from La Union and Pangasinan and from every other province in the North. It is not unusual for Ilocanos in the Philippines not to speak of a pros-

perous kin in America and for them not to talk of joining a
brother, sister, son or daughter in the future, soon, if it can
be worked out.

"For every three Filipinos you meet in the United States,"
quips a junketing official, "you can be sure to count four, not
three, and all four are Ilocanos." His explanation: one woman
in the group is likely to be heavy with baby.

Besides having a big brood or coming from one, the Ilocanos
are an easy group to tell. They plant *saluyot* in their backyard,
they store rice by the 100-pound sack. They get into heated
discussions about Philippine politics as if their lives still de-
pended on it. They speak Ilocano and persist in speaking their
"language". *Isu ngarud.* And why should it come as a surprise
if Americans pick a word of two of Ilocano instead of Pilipino?
And for Myra Waldo, author of a cookbook on Oriental recipes,
using *inapoy* for rice?

Next to them are the Visayans, those from the eight major
islands in the Visayas—Cebu, Negros, Bohol, Panay, Leyte,
Samar, Mindoro and Palawan. Like the Ilocanos they too love
the feel of their own tongue but because of divergent dialects
communication among them is oftentimes carried on in English.
They too are an easy group to tell because if they are not Os-
menas, Yulos, Madrigals, Magalonas or Rodriguezes they are
second, third, fourth cousins or something of the same.

Name-dropping is a pastime with them, pursued with no apparent effort to brag. "Did that fellow Locsin succeed in migrating to Australia?" "Did Ganzon switch to another party?" "Are
the Tiempos still in Silliman?" "Joe Rodriguez was here the other
week, didn't you know?" To the last question a number of other
names, nicknames, are given because in Cebu City alone there

are six such persons answering to the same name, each curiously, as solvent and capable as the other in making those sudden trips to America.

Inclined towards the less rewarding occupations, materially speaking, the Visayans in the United States are either musicians, music instructors, singers, painters, writers or film editors. They seem to possess a talent equal to their ambition for success, the kind that rates a magazine cover in Las Vegas, and the kind that draws critics from faraway Italy. But while artists by nature, they are not without their share of surgeons, engineers, lawyers, nurses and small-time businessmen.

The Tagalogs, on the other hand, have just awakened to the goings-on, along with the Bicolanos and those from Mindanao. And not wanting to miss any more of the fun, they too have started to move, stirring as much dust in the wake and causing position papers to be promulgated back home.

Actually, what provided the impetus was the U.S. Immigration Law in 1965. Under this law the Philippines — once good for only 100 immigrants a year despite parity relationship with America — can expect a maximum share of 20,000 from the annual pool of 170,000 reserved for countries outside the Western Hemisphere. Allotment is done on a progressive scale. In 1969, the Philippines was awarded only 13,000 berths (7,000 shy of the optimum outlay), in 1970 a little more, the reason being that after extensive research, study and consideration the number would just about maintain the ethnic balance of the Filipinos already in the United States.

The Philippines, in fact, has a good chance of getting bonus bites in the future, besides filling its share to the full, if countries in the Anglo-Saxon circle do not use up their "quota" (as was the case of Great Britain which left vacant a total of 50,000 places between 1965 to 1968). And if, it is believed, trade agreements and military arrangements between the Philippines and America continue to hold sway even after 1974, the year special relations between the two countries are supposed to officially terminate.

While the hypothesis on the special relations clause is conjectural, the matter on full allocation and bonus is neither far-fetched nor overly optimistic. There is today in America a growing need for certain saleable skills which can be met easily by allowing Filipinos to come in greater number. America is aware of this. In the reapportionment of allotment for the Philippines there is a tendency to favor people engaged in medicine, engineering and accounting and less of those in unrelated professions.

The non-preferred professionals, however, who manage to get through on the strength of a spouse working in the field of medicine, end up in banks, insurance companies and communication centers. The teachers with master's or doctorate's degree, obtained either at the University of the Philippines or at a provincial college, land jobs in training stations for retarded children or parochial schools in far-out places; some, not surprisingly, become matrons at Indian camps in South Dakota. The lawyers come handy as business conciliators or estate analysts, if glorified clerks.

Well-placed or not, they seem satisfied enough. They write home about the good life in America, to ask relatives to join them post-haste, to taunt friends, colleagues and townmates. Quite expectedly, they come as bidden — the accomplished, the well-bred, the influential, the well-to-do (see index), the brothers, the sisters, the uncles and of course the folks. They come to the big cities and the not-too-big-ones, determined and unstoppable, like lemmings on their march to the sea.

They come especially to the state of California, to such places as Oakland, Eureka, Yreka, Ukiah, Napa, Redding, Red Bluff, Chico, Marysville, Sacramento, Delano, Stockton, Salinas, Tracy, Paso Robles, Modesto, Fresno, Visalia, San Jose, Santa Barbara, San Bernandino, Santa Ana, Santa Rosa, San Luis Obispo, San Pedro, San Diego, San Francisco and Los Angeles. They gravitate to this mother lode state, where 70 per cent of the estimated 700,000 Filipinos are presently residing. They are here because the pay is good, very good, the highest in the world, and because, as they have been enticed in letters, the climate is Philippine-like in many respects.

The Filipino's first choice is California, talk of smog and grisly crimes and moves to depopulate that state notwithstanding. He is here mainly because it is, in the spiritual and physical sense, the closest he can get to home. Here he speaks Pilipino or his own dialect often enough. He gets his daily sauce of prattle and gossip — who is facing deportation and why, who stole a march with whom, whose birthday is up and so forth. And not too infrequently, he shares a jar of *bagoong* (preserved fish or small shrimps) and pieces of pickled fish and red eggs and shredded *gabi* leaves (a kind of vegetable passing as medicinal herb) with a just arrived countryman who, like him, is here very much for the same reason.

While still very much Filipino, insular in feeling and thinking, elaborately courteous, hopelessly clannish and generous to a fault, he has nonetheless succeeded in making his presence felt, as indeed he has. For although still belonging to a fledgling minority, struggling for recognition and respect, he has somehow achieved a status — that of being sought after and not simply tolerated or endured, of having, besides a lot of muscles on his back, the know-how and the conviction of his beliefs.

CHAPTER II

REASONS OTHER THAN ECONOMICS

The doctor, nurse, engineer, schoolmarm who leaves or must leave the old country does so between expectations and grave doubts, amidst huzzahs and not-too-flattering remarks. He is, by the very act of his leaving, actually neither a hero nor a heel.

To begin with no shining qualities of a hero are required of him to be able to secure a U.S. visa. All that a would-be immigrant needs is a driving endurance at patience, an untrammeled optimism, and plenty of luck — plus of course the standard requirements of four-to-six year college accreditation, a clearance from the National Bureau of Investigation and the Bureau of Internal Revenue, possibly a sponsor to guarantee his employment, a clean bill of health (lungs free of holes), and a one way ticket or the ability to pay the same — something like P3,000 by plane or P2,000 by ship (taxes included), depending on the prevailing dollar rate of exchange. A sizable bank account in the neighborhood of five digits is also required but then the applicant already wise to the ways of the hundreds and thousands before him gets past this with little difficulty. The slightly-dreaded interview conducted by a consular official comes as a routine. An applicant is yet to be turned down on grounds of defective diction, faulty logic or dubious disposition.

The main thing really is to get his papers processed, the sooner the better for himself and his overnight creditors — for did he not avail himself of the fly-now-pay-later scheme, touch friends and relatives for soft loans, more to cushion fears than to anticipate actual needs?

Between 1965 to 1968, the processing took only several weeks, six months at the most. With the flood of applicants seeking berth under the Third Preference status (the professional group) the wait has gone from months to years, with local measures and student unrest seemingly compounding the situation. A little ingenuity on the part of the applicant, however, may hasten his departure but such practice while generally resorted to is frowned on by Embassy officials.

Now, does all the leaving and wanting to leave make him a heel? Does his wanting to practice his trade, not in the land of his birth where his government had much to do with his acquiring a formal education and where he is repeatedly told that there is so much work to do for the doctor, nurse and teacher in the rural areas, constitute an indictment of the duly elected authorities? Prostitution of his profession? And lack of faith on his part for his own people? Does all this make him less a Filipino, and in effect an alien?

These are ugly thoughts that rear up at the back of his mind, lending discordance to an otherwise happy occasion. The feeling of estrangement is there from the time he submits his application to the time he finally takes off. These are things he must have to gird up for, alone and in private. For no matter how much he tries to shake it off, the sense of guilt, or what is, is never fully resolved in his mind, even long after he has left the country. Where did he fail his people? And having failed them — if he did — what is there to do, now that he is in a better position to be of financial assistance?

Prize-winning Poet Godofredo Burce Bunao, who claims to have "lost" three of his sisters to America and who like many other Filipinos in the Philippines would jump at the chance to join the exodus, has this observation to make: "The economic liberation of the Philippines lies in a big way outside the country — with the Filipinos in America. They have the means, judging from the lovely pictures they send and the glowing letters they write, and let us hope, the willingness, to take this challenge upon themselves."

The professional who leaves the Philippines for America does so essentially to improve his lot for what promises to be a lifetime opportunity. He leaves, and does, for the same reason a man leaves his rural surroundings for the big city, to have a little more of life, "to capture Heaven by storm", even if in so doing would mean acquiring ulcers and the American blood pressure and ultimately, as Thomas Woolfe puts it, not being able to go home again. He leaves, and does, for the Almighty dollar, what else, and not because he has lost feelings for his people and suddenly found faith in another.

The hurt of leaving eases up only — if it does — when he gets into the swing of life in the new country. For once here he immediately assumes a different stance. He becomes a more determined person, no longer the Filipino Poet Da Costa would ascribe as "soft, easygoing, parasitic . . . indolent, inefficient". While he would look up his sponsoring firm, cautious of making early blunders, he would keep an eye on other opportunities. Generally, he would settle for the job he signed up for back home before moving to a better employment.

Better employment in this case is not alone in pay and working conditions but also in being able to work overtime. In this respect, no individual is more overtime-prone than the Filipino professional. He is crazy about it and would as much forfeit pleasure and sleep than miss a chance to rake in more greenbucks. He will choose to work afternoons (3 to 11) or nights (11 to 7) rather than mornings, for what pay differential of $100 or so is in store for such shifts.

Moonlighting is another diversion sought with a good deal of interest. A school teacher will work as such in one place, then as clerk, salesgirl in another. A nurse or doctor will work full-time in a county, part-time in the city. An insurance agent will work undercover for two other companies. He seems to have within his small frame all the capacity and guile to be in two or three places 16 to 18 hours a day, seven days a week, with just Christmas and New Year and possibly his birthday thrown in for breather, without management of this or that firm, hospital or bank suspecting his multi-working schedule.

Every effort is expended in the name of the dollar — so he could have a lot salted in a bank, so he could afford the monthly payment on a limousine, and so also, he could have that house upwards the $40,000 bracket in a respectable area. It becomes an obsession with him to own at least an apartment, to have three cars in his garage and to acquire the other concomitants of modern living. After all did he not leave home and everything that stood for it, give up a life-time and risk being written off completely as borderline Filipino?

Professor Josefina Cortez, of the University of the Philippines, who made a study on "brain drain" at Stanford University concludes in her thesis that Filipinos come primarily to study and secondly to make a living. Which was so. Her assumption is based on Filipinos coming over before 1965, the year marking the preferential allotment from the old quota system. The accent has shifted since then from intellectual pursuit to material acquisition. The great to-do is making that fortune, or what to a Filipino is neat enough fortune. It has to be for the immigrant who must think of stability and feeding several mouths, of surviving in a distant land where he is told, time and again, that for a friend the dollar is the best yet he can have around.

There are of course other reasons why the professional leaves home. One is the prospect of a good marriage (for the single girl) or so she thinks; another is the itch for adventure, and still another the aesthetic search for growth, the head-in-the-cloud reaching out for fulfillment. Most often the girl with marriage in mind finds a mate soon enough, either through the usual method of attraction and distraction or the as-yet unorthodox method of the love machine. The adventurer discovers congeniality for his wanderlust. The artist finds expression, even recognition in New York, Las Vegas or Hollywood, which is to say getting into a show or landing the faculty list of a reputable school of music. The scientist: full flowering of his talent.

Some come for fancied reasons, like running away from something or somebody, to forget ingratitude and defeat, to expiate a sin, to free himself of a past. This place can be very ideal for the man and woman who wants a crack at marriage for the second, third, fourth, fifth and umpteenth time. Some come because a mother has chosen to stay put, or because an uncle is at last in a position to extend financial assistance. Some come to share a measure of glamor with a kin connected with the diplomatic service. Some come to prevent any talk of infidelity from going the rounds on the part of the wife or husband. Some come for unknown urge, and wished they knew why they are here, or why they were granted admittance in the first place.

The Gasmenos, Portugals, Marianos, Batongmalaques, Lagusays and Lingans are here to give their children "first class education". Drs. Estella Pacificar, Jose Soriano, Manuel Velarde, of Los Angeles; Drs. Conrado P. Ocampo, Alberto F. Laureto, of San Francisco; Drs. Adriano Agana, Lucito Gamboa, Nony Sablay, Isaias Sunga, of Chicago are here for a far reaching purpose: "to learn first hand everything about medicine, or at least on what we are specializing, so we could be of greater service to our people."

The single girl is in America to help brothers, sisters, nieces and nephews through college, to redeem a property mortgaged, no doubt, when she took up nursing. She is here to buy agricultural lands back home, to raise the standard of her family long deprived of stature. All these she accomplishes in the short span of two to three years, including causing a tri-level house to be constructed in the *poblacion,* complete with the latest in stereo phono, refrigerator, color television, projection equipment, oversize lamps, gooped up furniture — all made in and sent from the United States of America.

The single girl on a visitor's visa will go to some lengths to extend her stay, if not make it permanent. She will hire a lawyer for guardian angel. She will look up a solon for what a legislative rider can do for her case. She will go for a loveless marriage —

for the ritual of it — if this would mean achieving a goal, that of holding on to a good paying job or jobs and remaining in the world's richest country and in the country's richest state (California).

Cases of overstaying are nothing unusual with Filipinos. Those sent here to further their studies, make observations, cover important events or go on a sabbatical manage to become residents — even under pain of censure, court suits and bad conscience.

This is how much hold America has for the Filipino professional — how much sold he is to the place. Says a nurse: "My one day earning here is more than my one month salary in Manila, especially when I do a plus eight (over-time)." Which is no boast. A nurse's compensation for one day, over-time included, or that of any other professional, is more than the annual $60 per capita income of a Filipino in the Philippines. More than the monthly pay of some key-men in the Philippine government.

Indeed, a Filipino professional in America who saves enough in two or three years can talk of retirement and living it easy back home. It is mostly of this that he comes to America.

CHAPTER III

LOVE AT FIRST SIGHT

Regardless of background, persuasion or intention, the Filipino is likely to get his senses worked up to the hilt once in America. His first impression of the place is love at first sight.

And it is, as he sees all sorts of cars parked, moving or hurtling, neat and evenly-spaced homes, wide and well-kept avenues, wildlife unmolested on lawns, sunlight bursting through giant trees (Are these the sycamores and mulberries he read so much about — more than his own narra and apitong trees — while trying to divine a language apart from what he spoke in the house and the marketplace?). He will insist on hearing the din of cicadas at all times of the day even as he is being assaulted on all sides by the frequent thrust of jets and other sounds of escape. And quite true, as the billboards proclaim, Santa Anita is not just a racing track, it is a million flowers.

What strikes him most, however, are the very people themselves, the plain simple anonymous people he meets in the street,
the buddies he works with. He finds out soon enough that the
Joe or John Doe in America is not at all ugly, well, not the kind
written about or spoken of back home, proliferating in cheap bars
and boisterous at the sight of bellies rippling in feigned spasms
of sex. Not the Joe or John Doe who is likely to mistake a brown
man for a wild boar.

The John Doe in America is more like the Filipino Juan de la
Cruz in the matter of warmth, expansiveness and solicitude, only
with the former it is a little more, maybe because he has so much
to share or is it to throw away? Nonetheless, the American's willingness to help is immediate, instinctive. He will go out of his
way to lead a blind man cross a street or get inside an eatery.
He will not hesitate to pick up side-walk characters thumbing a
ride even when he is rushing to beat the clock and the traffic,
which is all the time, whether going to work or ferrying his children from school. He will give away prizelooms, chippendale sets,
mink coats, 24-carat diamonds, just to see how the gift will work
on the recipient. Crazy, yes, but the Filipino finds this every-
where, especially in provincial cities and lesser communities
where everyone is taken for a friend and ally, and not someone
to be wary of.

He too finds the American as great in sentiment as in humani-
ty. There is the case of an Irishman who, after having bummed
around a good deal, saw the need of returning to his country,
there to spend the rest of his years and to tread once more Grafton
Street (in Dublin), world-famed for its beautiful women. All
that he did was to tell his cronies about his plight. When he could
not be talked out of it a canister was passed around and that

evening, at his cocktail hang-out, he had enough for plane ticket and money to start him off in his nativeland.

Seeking out people in conservation comes naturally with John Doe. Although not given to pronouncing Filipino names, or any other names not American, John Doe is able to communicate in clear, cogent terms, even in Spanish. For Spanish is a second language in California and 12 other states. The Filipino professional is likely to welcome the chance of brushing up on the tongue without feeling self-conscious. He may, as some do, subscribe to Spanish periodicals. But this is being unnatural, if snooty.

He goes for American newspaper. Naturally. He is awed at the volume, the variety and the excellence at reportage. If he gets the chance to read, a habit he is yet to develop, he does so not so much for the events or the editorial contents as for the advertisements, except for items affecting Asia and the Philippines, or anything which has something to do with military and economic assistance, scholarship grants, Ben Arda's activities on the green, Ely Yares' title fights, Raul Manglapus' lecture tours, Corky's (Trinidad) syndicated cartoons (which is almost a daily thing in the big papers), the Benguet Consolidated Mines, the Miss Universe and Miss International contests, Ma. Teresa Calderon (the world's fastest reader), Senator Jose Diokno, Gen. Carlos P. Romulo and the not-too-pleasant stories of smuggling (which Consul-general Carlos Faustino tries hard to refute or minimize in print), quack doctor Agpaoa and threats of communist infiltration and invasion.

The ads, which, on regular days go up to more than 100 pages, say, for a paper like the *Los Angeles Times* or a picture tabloid like the *New York Daily News*, take most of his reading time.

If not absorbed in job offers, he is het up with possible bargain buys, missing as much a breakfast or an appointment. He is infinitely amused with new cars, priced as low as $69, for down payment; or slightly used ones for $400, or used cars for as low as $20, and on almost anything that can be had on easy installments and three-year-to-pay outcries.

He too is impressed with the candor and dispatch of John Doe. In applying for a job, all he needs to do is pick up a phone, inform the other party what he wants, and for how much — per hour. No effort is wasted on hedging or buttering up. No letters of recommendation are required, just plain getting on. If an opening, as advertised, has already been filled up, he is told right off, and no nonsense about it.

John Doe's efficiency at doing things is something, too, whether trimming hedges, tending automation or acknowledging letters. Road construction is done in a day's time, not months. Work while mostly routine and specialized at all levels could be downright boring, but so far the best system yet: the unexpected does not happen, not really, and the expected happens all the time, well, almost always, anyway.

Who said about disorder? Juan de la Cruz is particularly impressed with John Doe's adherence to law and order. Nowhere is this facet of American life more manifested than in grocery stores or at amusement places where people stand around in queues for their turn. Nowhere is obedience more evident than on highways and freeways where the slightest of traffic infraction could mean disaster of a giant proportion.

Juan is amazed at Jane and John Doe's seriousness at sports, even when just rooting for hometeams. They will reserve tickets a year or so ahead even for teams that are hopelessly cellar-bound. They will shed off their square trappings to be at a bleacher. Ladies past their prime will climb flights of rungs for the same. What he cannot seem to understand is why the average American, who works himself to the bone the whole five days of the week, would burn up his earnings for football, baseball, basketball or ice hockey in New York, Detroit, Chicago, Boston, Pittsburgh — a good 4,000 miles away — when he could have seen the game at no cost at all, in the comfort of an armchair, before his own television set. But, then, it is possible that John and the hundreds of other Johns, football or baseball buffs like him, hardly shell out a single cent for such out-of-town undertakings — somebody does, as in the case of P. K. Wrigley, chewing gum king and Chicago Cubs owner who picks the tab for such projects, to give his team all the assist in the morale-booster department.

Juan is further amazed at their capacity for going after what they want — whether skiing in Canada, cruising the Caribbean, spelunking, weighlifting or securing a seat for a play, concert or ballet. Could it be that they are impossibly restless? Or improbably fun- loving? Is this their idea of involvement, of a life lived fully and well, of "living a little extra?" Whatever the reason, the Filipino marvels endlessly at the Americans and America. He marvels at their sense of history, their knowledge of science, medicine and technology, their reading propensities, their almost sybaritic love of the sun, their compassion for animals. Here, a canine is a petted, pampered member of the family, not a *pulutan*, or a possible repast. Power resides in the people, not in the hands of a privileged few. A streetcleaner can expect action in seconds, from the police for a man shouting obscenities in a parking lot. The same streetcleaner can cause an auto repair shop to be padlocked for "shotgun" service done on his engine. There is a posi-

tive feeling of getting protection from the authorities, not intimi-
dation.

He is astonished at the Americans' ability to forget differences,
at their sportsmanship and trusting ways, their lack of arrogance
even in affluence and that sense of being law unto themselves.
The Filipino can, and does, talk back to his employer without
fear of reprisals. He can, and does, even after an exchange of
words, bum a ride with the boss' lovely wife or equally lovely
daughter, and what's so unusual about that?

These too are in his mind: Disneyland in Los Angeles, Marine-
land in San Diego, the Fisherman's Wharf in San Francisco, the
Statue of Liberty in Bedloe Island, the Old Church in Boston,
the Cabildo in New Orleans, the Curtis-Lee Mansion in Washington, Luther Burbank's experimental station in Santa Rosa,
the thundering waterfalls at Niagara, the glacial lakes at Yose-
mite, the awesome granite walls of the Grand Canyon, the rare
vegetation at the Mojave and Colorado deserts, the fern-car-
peted redwood groves in California, the rippling dandelions on
his way to Sacramento, and nature's other charms which America
seems blessed a thousandfold.

Quite poignantly, he remembers his first continental bus-ride
to the East, the snow flakes settling on his bare head while trying to beat, but not really, the traffic and the cold one late after-
noon in New York; he remembers waking up to the strange
crackle of icicles, the hot summer days in a stuffy room, the nip-
py air that sent a familiar chill to his body, stirring him into
weariness and reminding him of long nights and another winter
ahead.

America to the Filipino immigrant is the scent of apples in
an orchard and the sight of grapes, oranges and apricots redolent

in the sun. It is a bottle of fresh milk instead of tap water from a faucet. It is a house heavily carpeted from wall to wall, sweet-smelling and gadget-filled. It is cosmetics by so many names; it is soaking in luxurious bath bubbles and watching color television at the same time. It is applying chap-check and feeling feminine about the whole thing. It is drenching himself in cologne and applying deodorant at the genitals.

America is an indoor game of Battleship, Trouble or Aggrava-tion played unrelentlessly by both the young and the adults. America is having children in school and not bothering one whit about fees, textbooks, pencils, paper, erasers, transportation and sometimes even lunch money. America is opening a mailbox and getting a surprise-sample share of the latest in laundry and toi-letry. America is driving downhill on a convertible for a bottle of soy or vinegar overlooked in the weekly shopping list. America is being told about a cold, wet and windy day and getting exactly that, seldom the opposite. America is being warned about the excessive use of food additives for its glutamate contents, of cyclamates in soft drinks and the disastrous effects of smoking. America is walking the streets unafraid; it is sitting in a park and watching the sunlight fade on the grass. America is being in the shadows of the truly consequential, from Robert Kirsch to Gay Talese to David Doughlas Duncan to Jack Smith to Ernest Van den Haag to the Gordons (Mildred and Gordon) who aptly enough are referred to as the writers with the commonest touch.

America is a girl of three shaking a stubby but determined finger, and exhorting a bemused nurse that she won't do a thing like that, "drink my juice without a napkin". America is a fair-tousled little boy, monster or menace as he is lovingly called, bright-eyed and eager, coming to a children's party and answer-ing a question with a question: "What kind of bun would you want, young chap?" " What kind do you have?" America is young adults conducting teach-in for their teachers in summer, and young adults evaluating their tutors' performance at other times with such blunt, no-holds-bar comments as: "You may not be aware of it, sir, but your pants need a second visit to the tailor." "Why not a little grease on your hair and some of it on your shoes?" "You don't relate enough. You're too mystical, too abstract for our comfort." "Your level of instruction is too basic." "How about growing feathers (sideburns) on your face, for a change?"

America is licking a quart or half quart of vanilla or marbled ice-cream. It is cracking nuts the year round. It is nibbling *siopao, puto,* and *butchi* peddled around by fellow Orientals, not on foot but in coffee wagons or flashy cars, the latest. It is having something new all the time, and wishing for more. It is signing on dotted lines for almost anything purchased; it is, to some, borrowing money from a bank and thinking of working double time, so they can pay up fast and come back for more.

America is instant breakfast. Instant wash. Instant wear. Instant resolution. Instant fulfillment. Things are either useful or useless. Ideas that do not work out are instantly discarded; marriages that are not promising are instantly resolved in court, and this without having to make a trip to the divorce supermarkets (Reno, Las Vegas or Juarez in Mexico), or having to rig up excuses like adultery, cruelty, desertion, willful neglect, habitual intemperance and conviction of felony.

All that one party has to do — well, at least in the state of California — is answer two questions in the affirmative: Have you lived in this state for at least 90 days prior to filing the petition? Is your marriage beyond salvage? Whereupon, matrimonial bonds are cut off, dissolved, in less than a minute. The other party does not even have to be present. A corroborating witness is not even necessary. The low-down behind all this is that no one party is really guilty.

What, of course, is more astonishing to the Filipino immigrant is the fact that he is in America where he is treated beyond his expectation, despite the surge of nationalism back home and all the immediacy to revamp, reassess special ties existing between the two countries — with no one saying things behind his back, with no one coming up in querulous criticism why he is here in the first place.

CHAPTER IV

LEARNING BY EAR

Because a Filipino will always manage to have relatives, townmates and friends who will put him up on arrival, he will cash in on this to excess until he finds the need of moving to a place of his own—but only, after he has succeeded in ensconcing himself on a job.

Apartment-hunting can be a challenge to the man with a family. House managers will prefer dogs to children, which, of course, should not be taken as a reflection of their attitude towards the young, nor should it be understood as a residual feeling of the whites for the brown man. They do this to hold on to their tenants who prefer tranquility to mirth coming from youngsters. They do this to free themselves of legal problems arising from building hazards.

American laws while similar to Philippine laws in many respects can be strange, if quaint. A public official cannot refuse his salary on grounds of personal affluence, philanthropy or any such jazz. A buyer can change his mind, that is, rescind or cancel a deal within three days after he has made a down payment on a piece of real estate. A barber in California cannot charge less than $1.90, much less give a free hair cut, without having to go to court on a suit brought upon him by fellow barbers. A man can sue a neighbor whose dog barks unusually loud, get away with it, or so he thinks, anyway.

This actually happened: after obtaining a court order restraining a neighbor from keeping a pup in the premises, he found out to his extreme anguish that dogs are not the only creatures that bark. Dog-owners can do much more, besides, of course, providing the bite.

It is perfectly all right to carry a gun (Third Amendment—"the right to bear arms") but not a *balisong* or any Philippine knife or bolo. The point? The difference as to the definition of deadly weapons is purely semantics. Next to such expressions as capitalist pigs, making the orchestra, square out, meaning a guy in serge suit trying to look natural in a joint jumping with cats, the over-abused words or the most invoked ones are the Fifth and the Sixth Amendments. The former has something to do with a defendant's right to remain silent until a lawyer is consulted; the latter has something to do with the accused's right to counsel.

Laws are as much social as penal. A woman who stabs a lover to death can have the consolation of seeing the flowers she gives the deceased intact and undefiled. She can, if she so wishes, decide in consultation with the legal wife as to the kind of burial he should get, the kind he deserves.

What would generally constitute a simple case of *sub judice* in the Philippines is nothing but public opinion in America. During the trial of Commander Lloyd Bucher and the other 81 surviving crewmen of the intelligence ship, *U.S. Pueblo,* public opinion was vigorously sought to "ascertain" the innocence or guilt of the parties.

New words crop up by the day faster than he can grasp. He learns that the New Left has come to mean a group of young people, generally college students under 30 years old, advocating revolutionary changes in the political and economic life. It also means pursuit of freer moral code and new social structure, including mod of dress or undress. Its ultimate goal, seemingly, is *putsch,* seizure of power.

He learns that Charlie is not a good name to bandy around — it never was. The Negroes used to call the white man Mr. Charlie. "Then, after a few meals of corn mush," says Columnist Sandra Haggerty, "we got cocky and called him Charles." Today, Charlie has come to mean a Vietcong soldier. He learns that a stiff (this from a taxi driver) is a passenger who is hard on tips, used either way as verb or noun. Barrymore, once a magic name in the movies, is anyone with speech impediment. He learns that an exurb is a community smaller and farther from a city than a surburb. He learns that happening is a word used for a gathering where everyone becomes as much a performer as an onlooker. Doing your thing is an activity of the young which has something to do with annoying or afflicting the entrenched and the comfortable. The single girl learns that a fall is a woman's long artificial hairpiece, not one who has gone wrong. The single girl no longer takes umbrage at being addressed honey or sweetheart by total strangers. Superlatives like fantastic, wonderful, colossal, marvelous, tremendous, stupendous have ceased to hold valid meanings for him, hearing it said in trivia at all times.

Flower pot becomes earthenware vessel — it has to be in places where a check-up on marijuana is a must. Graduation becomes culmination day. Everyone is a specialist of some sort: a porter is a sanitation specialist; a cook, food specialist; a garbage man, refuse removal specialist. A farmer is known either as an agricultural engineer or livestock specialist.

Cash payment is not the same as it is understood back home. It is the total amount paid within a certain period, generally three to four months, for a set of furniture, trinket, stereo, television, gas stove or refrigerator. He learns to use such words as anti-hero (leading man in a play or movie with negative virtues), go-ape (to lose control of oneself because of excitement), fastback (a car with up-to-date finish). He is flattered to know that brain drain originally meant the excessive flow of highly educated and skilled people from Great Britain to the United States.

His non-white friends have a word for the rich white people moving out of a community to live exclusively by themselves — cliff dwellers, a name attributed in the beginning to descendants of Old Southern families. His teenage children pick words like zap (to kill), A-OK (great), hallocinogen (LSD), hully gally (new version of the frug). It is a semantical whirligig which he tries to keep up with.

Eighteen-year-olds and upwards are left very much to themselves, and so, between finishing college and working in an office or factory, the Janes and the Johns take readily to the latter, for the immediate reward it offers. The more ambitious work their way to college. The state and federal governments see to it that jobs are made available in summer or the year round for working students. Grants are kept open for students from low-income group (the official poverty line is placed at $3,533 for a family of four), and for those with academic or creative promise. But for all these incentives, not to mention the numerous scholarship funds offered by private institutions, notable of which are the Ford Foundation, the General Motors awards and the Los Angeles Times scholarship program, only one of five Americans in the age group of 18 to 24 makes it to a university.

Children of the rich and the moderately rich are still being marched off to Ivy League colleges for the traditional four-year course. Single sex schools in the East, however, have become anachronisms. The parents who expect to have a son at Princeton, Harvard or Choate (JFK's alma mater) or a daughter at Lenox, St. Paul, Mills Sarah Lawrence, Vassar and Bennington may well send their charge or charges to the University of California at Berkeley, Davies, Irvine, Los Angeles, Riverside, San Diego, Santa Barbara or Santa Cruz and expect as much result in instruction and co-educational experience.

Television, the Filipino finds out, shapes up the country's views on politics, military, couture, travel, current events and books, besides serving its chief function — commerce and industry. (There is one television set for every two persons in the United States.) What spare time the Americans have from their work, sports, commuting and the "idiot" box is devoted to reading or catching up on the more than 30,000 new books each year. Fiction is still the favorite fare. Next in line are books on visual and performing arts, history and adventure, culture, criticism, biography, autobiography and the biographical novel. An occasional forage on pornography or the op-pop-camp-kitsch-existential-occult-nihilist literature which comes with the junk mail, is not unlikely.

Americans know as much of William Manchester's latest literary effort as they do the current tailor designs of Bill Blass, Geoffrey Beene, Oscar de la Renta and Donald Brooks. They know O. J. Simpson, Joe Namath, Billy Casper, Connie Hawkins, Jerry West, Wilt Chamberlain, Elgin Baylor, Denny Mclain, Mickey Lolich, Tom Seaver, Lew Alcindor, Pete Maravich, Roman Gabriel — athletic supermen — as they Paul Newman, Barbra Streisand, Raquel Welch, Art Linkletter, Walter Cronkite, Bob Hope, Frank Sinatra, Moris Abram of Brandeis University, Artist Peggy Guggenheim, William Buckley, Jr., and the world's richest men: Paul Getty, Howard Hughes and Haroldson Lafayette Hunt.

No different from any other hero-worshipping people, the Americans however have a tendency of over-doing it to the point of idolatry. They will go to Chappaquiddick, Massachusetts, to fill vials with water or sand, or to gouge out shards of wood from the bridge made historic by the Ted Kennedy incident. A thousand books had to be written about the late President John F. Kennedy to meet an almost insatiable demand for the man. There are biographies of and autobiographies by individuals of solid and not-too-solid accomplishments. Stories of great achievements are held up for everyone to emulate or · approximate.

The motivational factor in America is a force the Filipino finds inescapable. It is not the simple getting by, but the purposing and achieving of great things. While he then works hard at what he originally came for, that is, to earn and save as much, he also tries to be something else, a do-it-yourself eager-beaver.

Involvement becomes his guideline. And thus like his American friends he achieves a comfortable sense of accomplishment, even if it is just for his own private world.

The Filipino immigrant, meanwhile, becomes the repository of secrets: "Imagine insisting on identifying us as Blacks when we are Americans like them." — this from a colored friend. "The nerve of them (the Blacks) wanting to star in variety shows and getting into our magazine covers." He ends up knowing every pettiness the white and the non-white have for each other, what the former should have done, what the latter expects to do once "truly emancipated."

The expatriate Filipino who has stayed long enough in America finds out that tonsorially his fellow nationals are still tops in the trade, that the best place to get sick or to have a tooth fixed, pasted or pulled is still the Philippines where the fee is very much within his reach, if not *gratis*. For who is the Filipino who does not have a doctor or dentist for a cousin, uncle or in-law — who did not have one for such a purpose?

The comedians are not just being funny when they crack jokes about the Greeks taking over the country, referring obviously to Spiro Agnew and Aristotle Onassis. They are not being funny when they say that everything nice that can be had in America comes from either Japan, Italy, England, Spain, France or Norway. Americans delight in having sweaters made in Japan, hand-finished combs from Italy, slacks, shoes and china from England, wood-carvings from Taiwan, laces from Denmark, ties from Thailand, little cars from Germany and perma shirts from Malaysia. They take pride in having a touch of the Himalayan way of life, or in having gone through two solid weeks of instruction and prayers, at six every morning, preparatory to a *shahada* (baptism) into Islam.

Another interesting aspect of American life is the white's wanting to take after the Negroes. First, they took to the weird dancing of the boogaloo, then they got themselves caftans and beads and dark glasses. Now, they are seen in Negro restaurants relishing soul food, one of which, the hog maw (pig stomach and intestines, likened to chewing on football bladders), the latter has long given up since their exposure to the more sophisticated cuisines.

Christmas and New Year, the Filipino finds out, are not exactly the kind of holidays he had wanted, even with his family around, well, not the kind he used to have back home, where for 21 days, from December 16 (start of the *misa de gallo*, early morning mass, to January 6 — Three Kings), he loses himself in piety and wayward pleasures. The Christmas holidays in America are cold and white and picture-card beautiful, all right, but at most one long countdown of commercial activities, strictly for the kids.

Church attendance, even on Christmas, is sparse by comparison. Only the old, those above 50, and the very young, under ten years of age, are seen around. Those in-between? It is possible that they are glued to a TV set for a crucial play-off involving a hometeam or an alma mater, if they are not in the game itself screaming murder at a referee. It is also possible that they have lost all enchantment with the church for the latter's passivity in the face of burning issues, namely, poverty and pollution and the Church's needless compromise of Christian beliefs and principles in the war against War itself. Thus, instead of going to Church, they find it more relevant to foregather in dank off-campus pads, doing what comes naturally, talking pot or organizing rallies.

Which is exactly what the Now Generation, or the New Left, is all about. They ask too many questions, and demand too many things. They want their voices heard. They want identity. Recognition. They want to have a piece of everything, from running a school to sitting judgment of judges to formulating the nation's foreign policies. They want to be 60 at the age of 16. They want understanding from their elders, not them doing the understanding all the time. They want their elders to understand, for instance, that there is nothing wrong with boys and girls living it up in dormitories and fraternity houses.

Parents are naturally baffled, worried. Laments an American father: "I worry for my son when he goes out of the house — I do more than that for my daughter — I pray."

The Filipino immigrant is leery about all this because very soon he too will have this kind of problem, if he does not have it already. He will have children wanting to fashion their own mold, instead of being molded and melded into a fashion. He will have children turning down job offers from companies with defense contracts and companies making money off of war. He will have sons worshipping anti-heroes, and daughters taking contraceptives before their time. He will have children rejecting the idea of divinity, and children insisting that God is really dead.

It is something he does not want to go through, but at which he must be prepared. Right now he can only hope that all this does not come his way. Like the American father, he can only pray that he be spared of such tragedies.

CHAPTER V

A PROBLEM OF IDENTITY

Many times the Filipino immigrant applying for work is refused because he has one too many college degrees. He is told in what in effect is a left-handed compliment as being too qualified or over-qualified. Confronted thus, he keeps the matter to himself. He talks of being an MA or Ph.D. only when a more valid reason comes up. A more valid reason in this case is nothing more than keeping up with a social club to which he must from time to time stand the scrutiny of his own countrymen. Other than this, a college degree in the humanities, earned either in a public or private school in the Philippines, can work to a disadvantage, can become a source of embarrassment for the unreconstructed professional. Nonetheless, because he must work for a living, he goes about the business of job hunting.

In seeking employment, dickering or compromising is hardly resorted to. He is told in the simplest of terms whether it is thumbs up or thumbs down. Oftentimes, a Filipino will insist at latching on to a job of his choice. When this happens he is told "to stop pushing people." He gets the message and instinctively moves on to the sides — hurt and not quite the same man with visions of paradise in America.

Nurses as a rule, however, do not have this problem. A nurse may work in a place one day, resign the next with the feeling that she will be up for grabs either at a clinic, a public service station, a convalescent home or another hospital. Private nursing in as much in demand, just as it is lucrative. The monthly pay for such service is in the neighborhood of $1,000, with option to bargain for more. If this is not enough she can apply for head nurse, supervisor and even chief nurse. Positions of this nature are daily advertised and not really filled. Similar opportunities are held up for laboratory technicians, nutritionists, engineers, accountants and even agricultural graduates. Besides good pay, they are assured of fringe benefits and long tenure.

Doctors do well in the East and the middle states where laws are less stringent and reciprocity is the thing. They become resident physicians and heads of departments. The more gifted are drafted to teach school with remuneration ranging from $20,000 to $24,000 a year. The Filipino doctor who sticks it out in the nation's state (California) does not stay very long as inhalation therapist, EKG technician, medical aide, laboratory technician, ambulance attendant or medical clerk. He eventually gets placed in a position of responsibility, if respectability, in a medical center in San Francisco or Los Angeles, where, again, salary items make up glossy statistics. Provided, of course, he meets all the state and national requirements.

The employment climate for a dentist, however, is not as auspicious, for all the talk at equal opportunities and corrective legislations. Local laws on dentistry and "union activity" simply make things very tough for the just arrived dentist. He either has to take a refresher course (16 hours a day, 6 days a week for one solid year), pass a set of licensure examinations (which many feel is like beating a dealer's hand in a plush gambling joint) or, he must by necessity work behind a counter or at some jobs more menial than medical. The same is true with the bachelor of arts, fine arts, philosophy, political science, foreign service and law graduate. A Filipino with such college background cannot be too choosy with jobs even in a place like California.

And what of the Filipino school teacher — the bachelor of science in education or the bachelor of science in elementary education or the master of arts in education — who laughed off a chance to be supervisor, principal or dean of a college? While validation of academic credits and permit to practice his trade is not difficult to secure getting the job he most wants or he feels up to is another thing. America is in need of teachers and teaching assistants, yes, but not, it seems, the kind bred and brought up in the "Islands." If a Filipino ever gets to teach it is generally in some far off places where the pay is sub-standard and conditions are reminiscent of wagon days.

Getting to teach and hanging on to it are entirely two different things. The Filipino teacher either resigns before his time, or accepts a library assignment. In certain cases he is immediately laid off, the cause being his speech, namely, his defective plosives, his shs and chs and his inability to open his mouth wide enough for the vowels. While passably well in grammar (a matter he is prone to exaggerate) he is not in diction, in the spoken word. His wards constantly shift ears to his brand of English. Thus before a nine-year-old or a twelve-year-old asks him in mischief or innocence whether he is speaking Yiddish, Latin, Russian or Swahili the Filipino school teacher takes the beaten path. He exits in a huff, and for a long time indulges in self-doubt, self pity and rebuke: " How come those tykes do not find faults with the French-American, the Canadian and the English whose accent is as thick and foreign as my Ilocano English? . . . Why did I ever leave home in the first place? . . . Why? . . . Why? . . . Why?

This makes him furious and sad and introspective. He begins to suspect that skin texture, build, height, origin, more than just speech, have something to do with his case. He becomes tribal and bigoted all the more. Nev r is there a need to feel Filipino than when the President of the Philippines, together with his wife and official entourage, comes over for an official visit. Neither is there a prouder occasion than when a poet-mayor in the person of Antonio J. Villegas delivers a heart-warming speech in English and Pilipino; nor when the internationally famous Bayanihan takes hard-to-please Bostonians by storm; nor when a boxer of Flash Elorde's dimension displays his wares at the Cow Palace (San Francisco), the Sports Arena (Los Angeles) or the Madison Square Garden (New York). The presence of movie personalities like Ronnie Poe, Jr., Joseph Estrada (also mayor of San Juan, Rizal), Luis Nepomuceno, Romeo Vasquez, Pancho Magalona, Zaldy Zshornack, Fred Galang, Marlene Dauden, Charito Solis, Susan Roces, Amalia Fuentes, or the prospect of Liza Moreno and Eddie Rodriguez coming around, is enough cause for a big scale celebration. So also is the presence of roving journalists like Jose Luna Castro, Joe Guevarra, Rodolfo Reyes, Joe Quirino, Sebastian Catarroja, Emil Jurado and the much-awaited visit of Nick Joaquin, Kerima P. Tuvera, the Linsangans, the Locsins, Max Soliven, Teodoro Valencia, Amelita Reysio Cruz, Tuding Guinto and Danny Villanueva.

But no reason is really necessary. Well-placed or not a Filipino will first be Filipino and something else secondly. Josephine Bowler Owen who left Albay province when still in her teens can embarrass anyone from that place with her knowledge of Bicol history and personalities (past and present), and her fluency of the regional dialect. She is too Filipino to be anything, in spite of her name, color and attachments to America. The same may be said of her brother, Frank Bowler, who curiously, because of fair skin and American ways, finds it difficult to be accepted Filipino among his countrymen.

But why should a Filipino who migrates to America, with plans to change his citizenship, if he has not done so yet, still want to remain Filipino? Simple, because there is nothing he can do about it. There is nothing he would want to do about it. It is in his speech (regardless whether his is good or bad English), in the pigmentation of his skin, his mannerisms, his desire to be seen in *barong tagalog* on occasions, his preference for *sinigang, gulay, kilawen,* his deeply religious ways, his very awareness, his hankering for ways Philippines and Filipino. He will write home for copies of geography and history books. He will order for stereo records — the latest of Pilita Corrales, Sylvia la Torre, Ruben Tagalog, Merci Molina, Carmen Soriano, Lynn Madrigal, Vilma Valera and Helen Gamboa. It is in his unequivocal choice of a Filipino for a wife, even if the whole affair is a total mismatch from age to attainment to attitude.

Everything boils down to a problem of identity, giving way to endless hours of soul-searching. For having left, did he not forsake a moral and social obligation? For what, indeed, is a nurse or a doctor if he cannot be around to administer the needs of the needy? What for is a teacher if he cannot be present any more to enlighten and inspire? What for is a leader in *ab-*

sentia? Is it having more of life for a dentist, lawyer, foreign service graduate working as clerk, taxi driver and such, thereby losing what little dignity and self-respect he has for himself, just to be in America? Is it having more of life not finding the love and respect he used to have back home? He cannot even have the simple obedience of a maid or a family driver because there is no such thing as domestic help in America. Not for him, anyway, who must try hard to survive, to come across with the monthly payment of a limousine or the second mortgage of a house, who must at the same time entertain the idea of making that fat savings.

The Filipino immigrant must then start an entirely different life, and does. For him, it is a question of picking up the pieces and beginning all over again, of a Ruben Eugenio quitting a deanship in Manila to try his luck in Los Angeles, of a Josephine Estrada forsaking her legion of fans in favor of another set of converts in the Hollywood area, of a Jo San Diego holding on to a job hardly equal to her talent, of a Ralph Benitez turning his back on a job in the *Manila Daily Bulletin* for something less in Florida. It is a life that is great on the surface, but hard-driving inside. It is, at the bottom, a constant search for identity. Identity?

Finding himself in a city of two to ten million people will entirely depend on himself — on how much he can manage to live *with* himself. Adjustment on all aspects calls for great effort. Acceptance is something he must work hard for. Meanwhile, he must fall back on his fellowmen "for that protective coloration of the crowd." With them, at least, he can have the acceptance and recognition he needs, psuedo or petty it may appear to be.

CHAPTER VI

SPEAKING UP

The Filipino professional who on arrival is immediately installed in a well-paying job, something like one thousand dollars a month, gets the feeling of being on Cloud Nine. Right off, he makes a down payment on a car in the $5,000 bracket — a weakness every Filipino is apparently heir of — and drives around in a two-hundred-dollar-suit and regards himself a world apart from his poor countrymen.

He talks of having a fleet of cars and a retinue of servants back home. He tells everyone that he did not really have to come — to make or to earn a living — because in the first place the rice-sugar-coconut produce in his plantation or that of his folks', is plentiful, and that he was head of a surgical department, dean of a college or things of the sort. He will rattle off names from President Ferdinand Marcos to Senator Sergio Osmena, Jr., to Mr. Nemesio I. Yabut to Congressman Fred Lamen to Dr.

Juan Salcedo to Dr. Hwang Yulo, without the title or tone of respect. He is likely to tell everyone that he has made a number of trips to America, and that he has seen most of the country, including Canada and Mexico — even if it were just the border cities of Vancouver in the North and Tijuana in the South. He is likely to say a lot more in an effort to impress.

Twaddle, twaddle, twaddle. Nothing but conceit and a compulsive desire to show off, a clear case of inferiority complex.

The Filipino immigrant, regardless of his calling, is a picture of naivete. He knocks off table spoons as he tries to help himself with a dinner fork. He picks up the phone every hour by the hour to talk to an acquaintance, townmate or friend, hardly suspecting that this hold-over habit from the Islands is causing a major distress to the host family, especially for long extended calls and calls that are out of town. He inquires where the nearest post office is, how much postage is needed for a surface letter to the Philippines, how much is bus ride, how much can be saved with a transfer ticket, what the social security card is for. The inquiries do not end with his moving to another place. He burns his line for things he must know about the house or apartment, e.g., what the thermostat is for, how the in-sink-erator works, why the flame (pilot light) continues to burn inside the gas stove even when not on duty.

The need to seek his own people is instinctive more than utter helplessness. The Berces family of San Francisco will hear Holy Mass at San Jose, a good 100-mile trip back and forth, just to be with the Bellezas. The Kiwases and Dagans of Orange County will make those weekly visits to Los Angeles just to be with the Buyagawens, the San Juans, the Tagas and the Respicios. The Marianos will make those periodic trips to Delano. Melba Orpilla whose nine children in the Philippines she is left to support, like many Filipinos in the same situation, will risk frequent plane rides just to be with a step-sister in Sacramento for a couple or days. The Reyeses will have a field day at the Nungas; the Balinsats will overstay at the Galpos and the Ecos and the Smiths. The Apolinars and Castanedas and Lopezes of New Jersey and Indiana will pile up in campers and station wagons for hours of bumper bumpering on the freeway, just to be with Filipino friends in Chicago and New York.

There is no better example of ecumenism in action than of the Filipinos in America. While remaining a Catholic, he will not mind attending a Protestant service if this would mean saving on fuel and catching up on the clock. He will not mind getting married before a pastor, or having his children baptised and confirmed Baptist, Anglican or Seventh Day Adventist and seeing them later on go to any church of their choice.

For diversion, he crowds around a table with newly-found friends for a harmless card game — if by then he has not succumbed to the American pastime of taking off to points of interest outside the city. The gambler has always a place to go to: Las Vegas and the Bahamas. If that is too much, he can, and does, get lost with Filipino, Japanese, Chinese, Hawaiian and Portuguese farmhands ("No *haoles* — white faces — around, please.") in the valleys, where he finds his way to some cockfighting (illegal in California and 46 other states), to the exasperation of law enforcing agencies and the Society for the Prevention of Cruelty to Animals.

Few Filipinos pursue the healthier and more profitable games for the simple reason that besides the lack of reach the professionals who are here came past their athletic peak. They are interested in sports all right but not the kind that will make them plunk down $3.00 or $7.50 for a seat that is "a mile away, anyway, from the scene of action," much less $30 or $50 for a ringside view. They will watch games on television from start to finish, from pre-game to wrap-up commentaries, the while gobbling chunks of spicy stewed beef and washing down the same with friendly booze, Philippine-style, half swearing into each other's confidences between commercials, about the good times they have had in the old country.

Meanwhile, behind closed doors and drawn curtains, the womenfolk busy themselves on square tables, bubbling away in-between *pong, panignit,* and *jai-alai* about famous and near-famous relatives they have back home. About land-holdings and heirlooms. About diamonds and "princess rings" (topaz, ruby and opal) acquired on their last sally to Hong Kong and Bangkok. What they avoid talking about though, except in jest, are ermines and satin peignor and imported maribou because even to the most discriminating Filipina such things can be extremely prohibitive, if immorally restrictive.

Gettng into each other's company goes all the way with the Filipino immigrant. A nurse will choose to work in a hospital not so much for proximity, difference in pay and fringe benefits as for the presence of friends and *kababayan,* fellow nationals. An engineer is drawn to a firm likewise, and so is the nutritionist and the accountant, although exceptions will always be made for prestigious positions. Holiday outings are planned in terms of groups, two or three families setting out to explore deserts and mountains and lakes.

In an effort to get matters done, the American way, he learns to speak up for things he wants, or must want — fast. In writing down a name or an address he does not play it by ear any more. He will ask the other party to spell out the word or words. Once cloying and patronizing he is now a picture of brand-new confidence and convictions. He will talk of priorities (family over country, or self over country) in an attempt to make his position in America tenable.

Drawn into an argument on love of country, he will readily side-step the issue, bristle with cliches ("Nationalism is a thing of the past, a racist concept, that's what." "Internationalism is now the thing.") and end up in a shrill note that national boundaries are only for dull-witted people.

While high on such beliefs, the Filipino immigrant, however, is aware that he is yet to belong. That corrective legislations, say, on housing, land ownership and employment — while plausible — cannot and will not change matters with him overnight. He must accept the fact that he is Asian, alien and non-white, the last used to designate the color group of Negroes, American Indians, Japanese, Chinese, Filipinos, Koreans, Hawaiians, Asian Indians, Malays, Eskimos, Aleuts, etcetera. He must accept the fact, and does, that for the present, he can only go so far as the immediate immigrant is allowed to — far enough for the Filipino with mostly the buck in mind.

Breaking into the upper strata of American society is yet to be achieved by him. He is yet to be a resident of Beverly Hills, Winetka, Bel-air or Cape Cod, or a charter member of civic organizations outside the ones whose membership roll is mainly (curiously) yellow and brown. The Filipino is yet to grace big social functions outside the ones he gives, and outside those he gets invited to merely for the purpose of showing guests, as in a country fair or a showcase window, how the *barong tagalog* looks, or how well the *balintawak* appears on his mate, or how skimpy the g-string is as a piece of garment.

For a fact the Filipinos have yet to get around as one cohesive body in order to be taken seriously, claims by those who actively work in the East and the West Coasts for the election of congressmen, senators and the President, notwithstanding. A federation that will tie up splinter groups existing in Hawaii, Stockton, Seattle, Salinas, Richmond, San Francisco, San Jose, Tacoma, Detroit, Chicago, Los Angeles, Washington, New Orleans and New York is yet to come by. A real community such as that of the Chinese, the Japanese, the Mexicans, the Port Ricans, the Bulgarians and those from the Balkan States is yet to evolve with the Filipinos in America.

He would like his countrymen, for instance, to flock to a Philippine Village for their common needs, instead of to places obviously put up for them by fellow Orientals. He would like to see them get genuine native goods at fairly reasonable prices, instead of substitute products, supposedly from the Islands, at sock-it-to-'em prices. He would like to see a Fil-American appointed to the U.S. cabinet, and a Philippine ambassador, consul general or vice consul drawn from within the ranks of immigrants. He would like to belong to just one group, one federation, and not to so many groups whose main reason for existence is assumption of professional and regional superiorities and bias imposed by religion, political inclinations and luck in life.

While many good things can be said of the Filipinos in America *per se*, including the oftenly maligned officials and employes of the diplomatic and consular corps, a certain degree of distrust seems to accompany every move that he makes when dealing with his countrymen or ex-countrymen. He cannot seem to entrust his dollars with them for any corporate venture. This is so because of defalcations heard or actual experience encountered, of being short-changed, and forking over too quickly five hard-earned dollars in membership fee to non-existing organizations.

Except for this minor activities at bunco, which definitely is not generic, the Filipino is a great thing to be. In a street, on a bus or in a crowd he will wink, smile or burst in Pilipino or pidgin-Pilipino: "Pa-r-r-re." (A street-corner way of greeting a friend, acquaintance or kababayan.) "Comosta, ka?" (How are you?) "Sa-an ka doon sa-atin?" (Where in the country are you from?) "Na hi-hirapan ka ba dito?" (Do you find it difficult here?) He will not hesitate identifying himself as a native of Iba, Zambales; Bulan, Sorsogon or Tagbilaran, Bohol. He will prevail on a fellow national, whether just arrived or long resident of the place, to come over to his house, to sample his cooking. "I've frozen bangus (milk fish) and fresh sampaloc."

One Cristobal David, of Pampanga and now a resident of San Pedro, California, was on his way to a beach market when he came upon a bunch of Filipinos with their usual litter of children about to partake of crabs and lobsters in an open stall. Sensing that they were his countrymen and that it did not look right to eat the stuff with just pieces of bread, minus vinegar, pepper and steaming rice he immediately introduced himself to the older members of the group. Before long he was helping them wrap up the food and hauling every member of the party to his place. He had rice cooked and other dishes prepared, making it a real holiday for both his adopted guests and his family.

Cristobal David is not a rarity. He could have been any other Filipino in America. For actually, time, distance and a touch of affluence have only made him more Filipino — hospitable and sentimental.

CHAPTER VII

WITH THE MINORITIES

The Filipino immigrant realizes soon enough that along with living it up with the whites a good deal of co-existence must be done with the so-called "culturally deprived" people of America, the Blacks or the Afro-Americans; the Latins, the Jews, the Chinese and the Japanese.

Immediately, his concept of fellow "Orientals" takes on a different light. Where before he thought and fully believed that he was the best of Asians, now he takes a more realistic, if dimmer view of himself, an apostate of a sort. For here he sees so much evidence of material contributions by both Chinese and Japanese. He finds out about this on television, or when he gets into a five-ten-cent store or a public mart or a million-dollar emporium.

The Chinese, operating in much the same way as they do

elsewhere, are well entrenched in the everyday business of buy and sell, whether import or export, wholesale or retail. They have their own chinatowns; the Japanese their Little Tokyos. Both run restaurants, markets, auto courts and motels, catering to as varied a clientele as can be imagined.

The overwhelming presence, if excellence, of the Chinese and Japanese in education and science is another thing, too, which makes a Filipino a little inadequate unto himself. A Chinese or Japanese will manage to be in the midst of scholarly and scientific research, but not a Filipino except in matters academic.

Both Chinese and Japanese have a healthy regard for their own newspapers which seem to function as chief purveyor, catalyst, rallying center and unifying force. There are dailies of this kind in every big city in America, while Philippine papers, whether English or Filipino, have yet to find their voice and following, and come out with the frequency of a daily, not weekly, bi-monthly or monthly. The dream of having honest-to-goodness papers, however, such as those of the Chinese and Japanese is kept very much in perspective. There is talk of starting a pictorial magazine along the *Life, Look* and *Ebony* format. In Los Angeles, there is serious talk to that effect, but it seems that the whole project will have to depend on somebody's husband, a mechanical engineer, also a Filipino, coming out of a war in one piece.

Meanwhile, the Japanese and Chinese are well ahead of any ethnic group in the over-all picture of activity. This is a fact the Indonesians, Thais, Malays, Ceylonese, Burmese, Koreans, Vietnamese, Laotians and the Filipinos themselves find little to quarrel about — something which even the highly cultured Germans, French and English will not dispute. Already the

Japanese and Chinese are spoken of as America's new elites, along with the Jews. And quite so because of status achievement in the occupational structure.

The Jews, like the Chinese and Japanese, are very much involved in the mainstream of American life — too involved, in fact. They are in business, arts, politics, science, everything. The Filipino immigrant, by and large, must have to deal with the Jews. If he is not working for them as doctor, nurse, lab technician, secretary, researcher or clerk, he is exposed to them in some other ways — the latter managing to hold the upper hand all the time. A Filipino has yet to work with a Jew on the same level, and not surprisingly, *for* a Japanese or Chinese entrepeneur. Either the Filipino has so much pride in him to work for another Oriental, or both Chinese and Japanese know him well enough to keep him just as friend and ally, not as employee or business partner. If he must work in Jewish-run hospitals or establishments, because of attractive pay, he must do just that, work the way Jews expect people working for them to do, with all the minutes and seconds accounted for.

But for this obstinacy, he finds the Jews very much like Christians, a comparison the latter will likely not find flattering. From them, for instance, he learns of such Truth as "If I am not for myself . . . who will be? If I am for myself only . . . what am I? If not now . . . when?" (Ethics of the Fathers — I: 11), or such edicts as "We are no longer alone, whether as an individual, as a family, as a community, as a nation . . . What is happening 'there' is happening here. Thus, there is no longer any such thing as poverty 'there.' It is poverty here. There is no such thing as oppression 'there.' It is oppression here. There is no such thing as ignorance 'there.' It is ignorance here." (University of Judaism)

He learns a little, in fact, of everything from other people, immigrants like him too. From a Laotian the Filipino finds himself defenseless when confronted with the fact that Buddha is also a Catholic saint, canonized and all, asserting that his official name is St. Jehosaphat. A Mexican friend tells him that the seed of an avocado is not to be discarded from the flesh of the fruit, when served, if the greenness is to be retained. An Osakan tells him that by way of saying "Hello!" or "How are you?" *they* say instead "How much money did you make today?" and if the hour is too early for that "How much money did you make yesterday?" A Mongolian friend explains to him that mongolism is not an ideology but a certain kind of idiocy. From a native of Swaziland, he learns that Mauritius is not the latest in liquor or hair spray "but one of the two newest countries in the world. I should know because my country was the other one admitted to the United Nations recently."

From the Irish he learns that *dinuguan* is nothing but blood pudding. The Latin Americans will insist on speaking to him in Spanish, as if in accusation that he has no business carrying around a name like de la Vega, Perez, Solis, Salazar, de Leon, Ocampo, Cervantes if he did not speak the language of Castile. The Chinese, on the other hand, wonder why the Chans, Tans, Syquias, Tanchocos, Tanbuntings, Dycocos and Yulos among the Filipinos are not Chinese-speaking too. "And why not Japanese? Weren't we in your country at one time?" — this from a Nippon jestingly.

He is taken for Chinese, Japanese, Korean, Vietnamese, Malayan, Indonesian, Polynesian, anything but Filipino. He does not seem to mind this except when it is his own countryman making the blunder, at which he shows a bristling irritation. He feels good, however, when mistaken for Iberian,

Chilean, Ecuadorian, Argentine or anyone presumably with better features. Whatever he is taken or mistaken for, he is lumped up with the Minority Group — which is good or bad. Good, when the talk is about achievements, regardless by whom — a Japanese scientist succeeding in propagating seedless melons on a commercial basis, a Chinese girl winning honors for a U.S. track team, a Cuban, Nicaraguan or Puerto Rican hitting home runs with the thoroughness of a Babe Ruth or a Roger Maris; bad, very bad when there is rumble in the streets involving little enclaves — knives brandished, bombs planted in vestibules — for then the thinking along this line is not of separate stratified levels, but minorities taken as one dark hideous mass of body.

Fortunately for the Filipino, though relegated to that class of people with Spanish surnames, he does not feel and think of "two souls, two thoughts, two unreconciled strivings, two warring ideals in one body." He does not talk of rage and racism, only about friendship and greatness and glimpses of ecstacies.

The dilemma of the black man is not necessarily the dilemma of the brown man. With the Filipino, it is not so much being right, as being *here*. Militancy is not his thing. The Filipino doctor, engineer, nurse, bank clerk, teacher steers clear from any arguement that has something to do with racial differences and mystiques. He refuses to be drawn into a vortex of sympathy for what the Blacks call the "nobodyness and the acute ache and anguish" of having to live in so many situations.

He has enough troubles of his own, says he, to bother with other problems seemingly not his. This, of course, does not mean that he is without the potential of joining protest marches and the like, that he is oblivious to the cries of "physical life amidst psychological death," on one hand, and the unspoken shame and burden which the Whites must take up and bear through, on the other. But because he is caught in a situation where silence and prudence would make more sense than articulateness and active involvement, the Filipino immigrant does just that, not taking issues.

Understanding the Black-White confrontation, however, is a necessity the Filipino undertakes for himself, and does. For living successfully with the Whites and the other groups of people in America is as important as living with the Negroes, which today constitute 10 per cent of the population, or roughly 22 million people. They too are doctors and nurses and engineers and teachers and clerks and orderlies, whether anybody likes it or not.

The Negroes confide their secrets and fears to the Filipino because of a feeling of geographical belongingness and a parallelism in the Brown and Black history, and because they see the high visibility of their color tapering off with the brown man's; black, as it is, so they say, coming in all shades of brown.

To which, neither confirmation nor rejection is offered. The Filipino holds his ground of neutrality as when he first came, committed only unto himself and to the cause for which he came for. The Filipino keeps the peace to himself, wishing he had the full right to ventilate his views on any subject, directly or indirectly affecting him. But, again, his main interest in America prevents him from participating in matters seemingly not his own. He, therefore, accepts what comes. He listens and watches a lot, an onlooker even at happenings.

CHAPTER VIII

INTO THE MAINSTREAM

Unlike the Black man in America, the Filipino is not resentful of his state. He accepts the ambivalent life he must lead. In his home he is still the same Juan de la Cruz who left Ilocos, Tarlac, Bulacan, Bicol or Visayas years ago. He adorns his place with native carvings and paintings, Amorsolo or H.R. Ocampo originals, or oversized family portraits, anything that will remind him of the folks and the old country. The piano, once a status symbol in Philippine homes before it was eased out by the stereo and the television, is still the thing in the living room. A pool table sits somewhere else too prominently in the house.

The feeling of being Filipino is indestructible in him. Dr. Apolinario Reyes will risk burning a finger to have *lechon,* broiled pork, on special occasions. Esther Calleja-Berces, an immigrant of twenty years standing, will scrub herself clean with a stone picked from the foot of a live volcano in the Philippines, instead of a plastic bathbrush manufactured in Los Angeles. Paul Quintos will tickle his backyard into smiles of patola, sitao, camote, eggplant, malungguy, sayote and saluyot — wishing the same for the papaya, mango and other tropical fruits.

He finds the need to eat *pinakbet, adobo, sinigang, escabeche* the rustic way — with hands, not spoon and fork, and with one leg limp on a chair, or both legs crossed in half-lotus position. When entertaining foreign guests, he goes cosmopolitan: lamb chops, abalone and tripe cooked with such condiments as yogurt, parsley, scallions, anchovy paste, sassafra leaves and turmeric, and served with table wine before, during and after dinner. If he must play his newly-acquired phono it is generally Philippine or Latin or mediterranean music — and as expected at jukebox throttle for half the city block to hear.

Outside his house or apartment, however, he tries to be another Juan de la Cruz, even in the simple act of dumping garbage. He puts on somehting proper: street clothes and shoes, not undershirt or pajamas and wooden clogs. While wanting to do things his way, as he was prone to do back home, climate and culture prevent him from doing so. He must wear working togs in summer, gloves, bush jackets and trench coats in winter. He must acquire a set of clothes for all the seasons of the year. He must learn to grab a sandwich, to eat plastic food, to do things at a fast clip, the while remembering to say the proper word, shopworn and meaningless it may seem to him. He must submit and does, inevitably to things American. What reservations or misgivings he has about the new life, Juan de la Cruz buries it at the back of his mind, or airs it only to his own countrymen or ex-countrymen.

In the Philippines he did not believe in putting money on insurance, not especially after the years following the collapse of local mutual companies. The only kind of insurance he believed in was money saved in a bank and money lent to a peasant, generally P5.00 apiece, for a 44-pound sack of palay he gets in return at harvest-time. Here Juan gets a different picture on investments. He becomes receptive to the idea of insurance. For here insurance is written into the law. If it is not in some cases, somebody is bound to sell him one, anyway, on his car, house, savings, title of his property, even on the practice of his profession.

Salesmanship is as much a skill of persuasion as it is a science of endurance, of wearing the party down by mail, phone or the face-to-face approach. It is organized, thorough, crafty, clobbering. It hits where it most hurts — the pocketbook — not with one lethal blow but with imperceptible peckings extending for a period of years. Juan de la Cruz is yet to find a way to resist American salesmanship, not that he would like to resist owning a new television set or a new car from year to year, or a house and lot at a real bargain, "with no down payment to speak of." Not that he would like to resist the promise of comfort and security in old age and the great life that insurance can give his beneficiaries.

And, not that he would like to resist time-honored institutions. In the matter of credit, for instance, the Filipino will get a car on installment even if he could have paid cash and saved money in the process. Back home a credit is a family secret. Here it is something to crow about. It just does not seem right or usual not to be able to obtain things on credit. For the line of thinking on the matter is this.: that he has either the cash, which is unlikely, or that nobody trusts him enough, which is likely. In keeping up with the system therefore Juan sees to it that he avails himself of every credit facility, from gas to grocery to services (and soon to church tithes, too). He stacks up himself with as many as two dozen credit cards, the more the better for his ego and corporate image.

In an effort to be understood, to sound American, or is it English?, he will lose himself in a speech pattern, and does, happily or unhappily. He will pick up words and expressions, hardly caring whether the same is dialectical, obsolete, arcane, slang or foreign. He will put on affectations, speak through his nose for sounds that are not nasal. Acacia, normally a three-syllabled word, becomes a-h-k-sha; short sounds become generally long, and a strong shift of accent from second to first syllable is suddenly noted — giving him cause to doubt whether he was tutored properly in the phonetics or that, maybe, he is hearing things incorrectly said.

When he first came he sported a crew-cut hair or one close to it. He prided in being clean-shaven. Now he grows it long, Biblical-like, with something of the late sixties and early seventies added to it: the sideburns. (He would have loved a beard and mustache if such facial feathers grew well on him.) His taste for clothes, colorwise, becomes mod. And while nodding in approval to every fashion upheaval, Juan would much prefer having his coat and trousers tailored in the Philippines where it is inexpensive and more to his likings. Although a more valid reason for such preference is that Juan hates the idea of having to pick his size from the boy's department.

Like almost every one in America, rich or poor, young or old, Juan learns to do everything by himself. He learns carpentry, masonry, a little of plumbing and barbering. He cuts the hair of his children and that of his wife. He even learns to cut his own — an activity he would never have tried back home but at which, in America, he finds a necessity and less cumbersome than having to put up with a barber who is not a *kababayan*. He does not regard baby-sitting a feminine task any more, nor does he mending and marketing. He learns to wash clothes, to dry-clean woolens, which, after all is no effort because all he has to do is drop a quarter in a slot, if by then he has not yet acquired his own washing and drying machines.

It is inevitable not to know about machines, because whether at home, in the office or in a hospital (where more than 50 per cent of the Filipino professionals earn their keep) he operates, manipulates, tinkers, talks, listens to and takes orders from machines. Technology has made it so simple and convenient that a nurse, for example, will get all the information she wants about a patient, and about the type, dosage and frequency of medication needed, by simply inserting a film cartridge into a computer. She will ask the same machine for a full and updated report on the patient, even chances of complete recovery.

And because it is also imperative that he updates himself on other matters concerning his work and the world at large Juan eventually develops the habit of reading. This time he goes beyond the classified pages. If he must look up advertisements it is no longer for a car or a stereo or places to moonlight, but for books he can read and add to a growing library. A trip to a bookstore, grocery or supermarket usually ends up with him lugging home a volume of an encyclopedia. He goes back for the succeeding volumes, week after week, until he has the whole set to himself, and until it is time a start a new collection. Or, as in the case of Webster's Twentieth Century Dictionary, until he has the complete works — the whole 2,432 pages — ready to be fastened between hardbound covers. Back home such acquisition would have been almost impossible. Provincial schools would make so much as a fuss looking up congressmen or holding benefit shows and dances just to raise P800, the cost of a standard dictionary. Here he can well afford the giant Webster's, as he can other things beause the huge book like other commodities can be had on a run, that is, purchased through several weeks or months of piecemeal payments.

Indeed, Juan learns to catch things on a run because everything *is* so: piecemeal, experimental, tentative. Everything is installment plan and "magic formulas" and "new concepts." Everything is a leap forward, towards the better life. Which fact, of course, modify his thinking, recast his values, improve his outlook. Where before, for instance, he will do a number of things for *palabas*, show off purposes, to please other people and to effect a good image of himself, now he does things mostly to please himself and secondly, if at all, to please others. He is not as gravely concerned any more about what other people think of him as what he thinks of them.

He learns to put a higher value on the material more than the spiritual, on the essence more than the form. Where before he would ask "Who are you?", now it is "What are you?" He becomes epicurean rather than stoic, active rather than passive, pragmatic rather than abstract. It is in terms of now, not yesterday, of looking into the future, instead of looking back into a past. Like the people around him, he seems to thrive best under pressure for what, machine-like, he must continually produce, produce and produce. With science seemingly on his side, he talks of inhabiting the world and the stars in a life span of centuries — "so why bother about yesterday. There is so much living to do now and the next hundreds of years."

But for all the talk of penetrating the mysteries and conquering the universe in his lifetime, the Filipino immigrant must, as he does, harbor new fears. It is not the fear of losing a job because he knows there will always be a job, or jobs, for anyone wanting to work, for anyone with qualifications. It is not the fear of having nothing in old age because that too is taken cared of in welfare aids and social security, but it is the fear of losing everything in a twinkle, either to man or nature.

It becomes clear to him now why on coming as an immigrant he was handed a blue pamphlet at his port of entry underlining his main duty and responsibility, namely, to report any person or foreign government who contacts him for purposes inimical to the interest and security of the United States of America. Now he understands why a little rain or a little gust of wind or a little shaking of the ground is regarded with great alarm. He understands, or so he thinks, why a high premium is placed on every individual person even if such person has pleaded guilty to a crime of, say, first degree murder.

In the past he laughed off such perils as the *Huk* menace (pocket activities of the communist), the tropical furies packing winds at 120 miles per hour, and earthquakes at intensity eight. Now he is scared of rifts and calamities, even in the knowledge that such events are merely dramatized, for the most part, to awaken the people from their relaxed and apathetic attitude, so puts a humorist, in order to keep the sale of liquor, aspirin and tranquilizers going.

He is terrified at anything that is a threat to his life, family and property. But such fears, founded or not, only quicken his pace, serving him well to get into the American mainstream of life. He falls a little behind the line only because of the dual life he must lead, the dead weight he must carry, like the re-membrances of home and his tacit reluctance to accept every-thing western — to go totally committed. Otherwise, he is as good as the inhabitants adopting him, as liked and wanted as any.

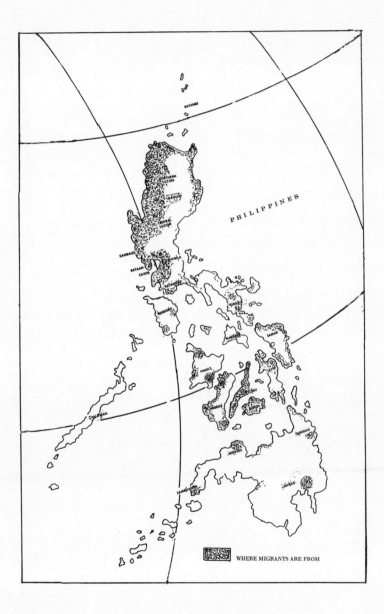

PHILIPPINES

WHERE MIGRANTS ARE FROM

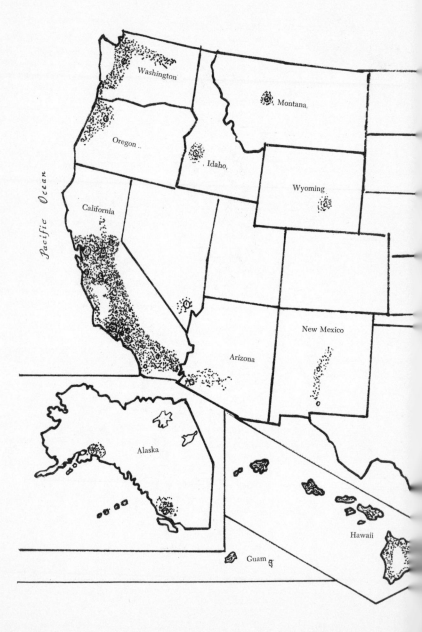

UNITED STATES

Michigan

Iowa

Illinois

Massachusetts Connecticut
Rhode Island
New York

Pennsylvania

Washington, D.C.

Delaware

Virginia

Atlantic Ocean

Louisiana

Florida

Gulf of Mexico

WHERE FILIPINOS ARE AT
(BREAKDOWN NEXT PAGE)

─Filipino Population in U.S.A.*──

California	475,000
Hawaii	103,000
Illinois	20,000
Guam	15,000
New York	14,000
Washington	12,000
Louisiana	11,000
Oregon	6,000
Washington, D.C.	5,000
Connecticut	4,000
Nevada	3,000
Pennsylvania	3,000
Massachusetts	3,000
Rhode Island	2,500
Arizona	2,500
New Mexico	2,500
Alaska	2,500
Florida	2,500
Other States (Delaware, New Hampshire, Maine, Texas, Wyoming, Montana, Idaho, Virginia, Michigan, Iowa)	15,000
Total	701,500

*Figures based on estimates supplied by consulates and community leaders.

PART TWO

AMONG COUNTRYMEN AND EX-COUNTRYMEN

CHAPTER IX

THE FARMHANDS

One group of fellow nationals the Filipino doctor, nurse, engineer runs into not long after he has settled down in America are the farmhands, referred to in trifle as OT's, acronym for old-timers, or *damatan,* Pilipino slang for the same.

Elderly but still energetic, they move about in vintage cars and clothes of their generation. If they are not making the rounds of beaten spots in a city, an activity they do not seem to tire of, they are fraternizing and shooting pool with countrymen and ex-countrymen, and promising them clusters of freshly-picked grapes, heads of cabbages, crates of tomatoes and eggplants — the last, obviously, said after several rounds of beer.

They will make alibis to be in the company of a recently arrived, get him or her to say yes to an invitation. Once acceptance is given, they will go about notifying friends within the neighborhood of 50 miles for a *salo-salo,* get-together, they are to give (generally at a friend's or relative's place) for the "cousin," "nephew" or "niece" just come from the Islands. The response is quick. They come eager and curious.

The cousin, nephew, niece is then shown around, and like one being honored he tries to look his part — with elan. He smiles, bows, shakes hands, remembering to say *po,* sign of respect for elders, from time to time.

In the inevitable question-answer period that follows he succeeds in generating wide-eyed interest as he tells them of the tight money situation back home (old hat as that may be), the strides taken by the Philippines in nationhood despite attendant problems of growing up. There is disbelief and laughter as he tells them of the Zamboanga monkeys, believed to be the country's singular contribution to the U.S. space program. There is nostalgia at the mention of religious processions and of barefoot flagellants walking on hot dusty roads.

"What came out of the land settlement in Mindanao?" "How much export do we make each year?" "Have we finally balanced our trade?" "Whatever came out of Asis and Antillon?"

"Bakit, sino sila?" (Who are they?)

"Didn't you know? Asis, Ricardo Vinzons Asis, is a Filipino who had a couple of poems in the *Atlantic. The Atlantic Monthly.* That was about 20 years ago. Antillon, Johnny Blanco Antillon, was a hit in the big town. He was here on a youth program sponsored by a newspaper in the East — was it 15 or 20 years ago? Anyway, his speech at the United Nations, one of many he delivered impromptu, was printed in full by the *Digest. The Reader's Digest.* I have not heard of them since."

"Do you happen to know Ricardo Marcelino and Remigio Young?"

"Well, not personally but I know them to be cinematographers, two of the best in the craft, I understand."

"Is that so? Well, during the Depression *Mang* Andoy, that is Ricardo, was in business all by himself. He made cut-out paper profiles of people who would pose for him in the Hollywood area. Miggie had a more interesting job. He worked in a brassiere department of a film company."

"Did you leave the country because of fear of Communist invasion?"

"No, no, *ay hindi, po.*"

"Is there danger for the Filipino going communist?"

"Not a chance" is his instant reply. "He detests too much authority. He is too religious. He has too much sympathy for the poor and the downtrodden."

With a niece (lady teacher, nurse or doctor) the talk is not about communism, brassieres, bare-foot flagellants and monkeys. It is about money saved, cars acquired and single- blessedness endured through the years. A sample of such talk runs something like this: "I have a Studebaker and a Packard, not to mention $5,000 in the bank. I will do anything to have a Filipina for a wife" — from man number one. Man number two: "That's nothing. I have three cars, all in running condition, and a savings of $10,000 in cash and bonds" — an obvious lie. Man number three: "True, true, perhaps, but all of them have had three or more wives. In my case I've been married only once"—partly true. Man number four: "But most of what they have, *Inday,* goes to alimony. I'm a widower. I'm free. What's more — I'm Visayan" — a little convincing, perhaps, until man number five blurts out: "But he's a welfare case, *Neng*." Whereupon there is shuffling of feet as man number five is cooled off to a corner.

Trouble is averted only when the lady makes an exit, half-admonishing them as she does in Pilipino and English: "*Bakit ba tayo magaaaway away?*" (Why must we have to fight?) We're friends, and that's what I'd like all of you to think of me, simply as a friend, nothing else."

This does not end there. After this abortive meeeting the farmhands make real efforts to look her up. They bring flowers and gifts; they swear to her of undying love. *Tiaga* (patience suffered through humiliations) sometimes gets its due. The "bachelor" with the least experience wins out. Which means that a hurried divorce is sought by the Pinoy still likely tied up, and marriage is pursued with immediacy.

Marriages of this nature are not, however, everyday occurrences. A nurse, teacher, doctor would rather remain single than be caught "dead" sharing bed and board with a "grandfather." She is emphatic about this. Fierce.

The Filipino farmhands who then must have someone from home and who now must do so for still another reason, after repeated rebuffs, make that long overdue trip to the Philippines, where they immediately hie up to their towns and barrios and go about the business of wife-shopping.

This reached high tide five to ten years ago. Farmhands in their fifties and sixties headed for home, and came up with the luxury of country maidens thirty to forty years their junior.

The tide has ebbed out since, and not because they have lost love and interest in the Filipina. It is just that things have become more cumbersome and expensive. The dowry has gone up from heads of cows and carabaos to modern-day chalets. And the matter of squaring it off with the various agents of government for that trip back, with a spouse, has become more prohibitive.

The need to have Filipino women nonetheless continue to remain as much their obsession as age-old plaint. Says one: "We would not have led miserable lives, nor drifted needlessly from one shoulder to another, if, in the beginning, our women came with us, stuck with us, and saw us through. But what really happened was that they stayed home. They had to be with the folks. Unlike other women who kept up with their men, and followed them wherever they went, our women stayed behind, too scared of a life away from home. They were too timid for their own good. As a result, we saw no point in growing roots — in making a home for ourselves."

During the cold months the Filipino farmhands move around in Arizona and New Mexico. Spring sends them bunny-hopping to Coachella Valley, and to Bakersfield, Orange Cove, Fresno, Los Banos, Gilroy, Castroville, San Jose, Salinas, Portland, Tacoma, Seattle, thence to Alaska. The Ilocanos concentrate for longer periods in Arden, Lamont and Delano; the Visayans in Stockton and environs, the hardier of the two in the Alaskan region.

The time pattern hardly varies: they will stay for one or two months in one farm, another couple of months in another, simply to pick the harvest or to assist in the canning of goods. They cannot seem to find the patience for tilling the soil and tending the plants any more, much less for staying around in one farm longer than one season. They are for getting out fast, to see what is *mas mabuti* (better) in the next town or farm.

Moving around is as basic to them as making the buck. They are for going after fair game, for dealing out cards, for extroverting—which facts explain a good deal about their bar-room morals and gambling den manners, their courage and posturings in the farm and on bargaining tables.

For not surprisingly, they too are organizers and strike leaders. They are known to have started a lot of causes. But durability and consistency of efforts are not among their stronger points. They seem to lack the waiting quality, the follow through and the tenacity of a Cesar Chavez. As a result, the other fellows taking over get all the kudos. The Filipinos get the brunt of the blame for what they initiate if things do not work out well — which is often.

Their intensity seems undiminished for pleasure and knife-wielding activities. They will get into fights for a fellow country-man, cast aside reason for *amor propio* (personal honor). They will stake a whole month's earnings on a pair of rolling dice or on some undulating hemlines — anything that will give them the "kicks."

But behind all this is the simple craving for a normal life — wife, home and children. Family life, however, while pursued at all times, is more apparent than real. It becomes a reality only when they meet mates for whom they can have the truest feelings. When this happens, they forsake their gypsy-like ways. They move to urban areas, get themselves jobs in kitchens and dining halls and sweatshops. Or, they remain in the farm, this time as year-round workers or small-time owners. The more resourceful become personal valets, studio grips, sextons or proprietors of seedy barbershops.

But short of honest-to-goodness mates they will bunch up in

farm camps, play gin rummy, regale each other with stories of adventure and misadventure. They will sing old railroad songs. They will follow the crops, and know every farm and farmer in New Mexico, Arizona, California, Oregon and Washington. They will cook up strikes and boycotts, lead it for a while before leaving it off to the other guys. They will do the city, make friends and shoot pool. They will even come around with those crates of tomatoes and eggplants, not so much to keep a promise as to prove that they were not really drunk the last time, only a little inebriated.

The farmhands will establish kinship with the just arrived. They will invite him to a *salo-salo*, not just once or twice, but thrice or four times over. It is to them after all an attempt to forget sordid experiences. It is to most a renewal of a promise. A restoration of the soul. A way of making up for failing to send brothers and sisters to school, as promised. For not having gone home to visit the folks, while still alive, in spite of entreaties from relatives.

CHAPTER X

THE CITY OLDTIMERS

The Filipino oldtimers residing in cities are as much conspicuous as the farmhands, even for their relatively small number. They drive second-hand cars, and are seen in clothes a little behind the times. Both speak unmistakable Filipino English, a halting Pilipino, but fluent Ilocano or Bisayan.

The city oldtimers, however, are not as irrepressibly enthusiastic as the farmhands. The latter will smother the newcomer with pleasantness on first encounter, the former will remain civil and correct for sometime.

The explanation seems to be this: the farmhands, mobile as they have always been, go to places simply to live off their wages; the oldtimers, who have families to begin with, stick it out where they are, preoccupied. The farmhands must hope for love, family and home; the oldtimers must try hard to keep up with their Caucasian neighbors — which means long hours on the lawn or yard and tidying things in the house.

A more credible explanation seems to be psychological. The "citolds" (diminution for city oldtimers) find it hard to believe that the newly arrived can have it all to himself in so short a time — good job or jobs, flashy cars — things which took them all their lives to achieve. They find it hard to accept that he should be ahead of them. Thus, this nudging estrangement.

The just arrived gets the feeling of rejection. He cannot talk of academic preparation and training, job offers and moonlighting without him turning them off. This is not to say that the oldtimers are lacking in college background. In the thirties and forties they supported themselves to school by working in hotels. They lived in old houses, the Ilocanos with the Ilocanos, the Visayans with the Visayans. But even with impressive credentials, they never rose higher then chefs or maitres d'hotel.

The passage of the McCarran-Walter Act, while making them eligible for U.S. citizenship, was no open sesame for the kind of jobs they had worked so hard for in night schools. When this law was enacted, in 1952, many of them were way advanced in years, and at that time the Filipino image in America was barely that of nurse-doctor-engineer-clerk-insurance agent which it is today. Seeing the just come, although conational, obtain better jobs only made matters worst.

The Filipino doctor, nurse, engineer understands that. He understands, for instance, why the oldtimers must regard him with apathy and suspicion, why they must want to lord over the council affairs of every Filipino community, be it Honolulu, Hilo, Waipahu, Maui, Seattle, Portland, Vallejo, Stockton, San Jose,

El Camino, Yuma, San Francisco, Los Angeles, Chicago, Washington, New York.

Unlike his experience with the farmhands, this time he does the seeking, the *pakikisuyo* and the *pakikisama*. He looks them up several times.

The first meetings are generally superficial. In between attempts to sound cordial, the newly arrived must hear of such expressions as "you reaping the fruits of what we planted and not showing any gratitude for it," "we trying very hard to put up with your insufferable arrogance," "the gall of calling us mental epileptics" and taints of the sort. All this, of course, are said in an effort to assert themselves, and to exact the respect (obedience) which they feel is due them.

There are second and third meetings, depending on how much he had agreed or politely disagreed on, or how good a listener he had been. For far from being sensitive and surly, the Filipino oldtimers are about the warmest elders he can hope to find. They will insist on having the liquor drained to the bottom, and wrapping extra food for his family. They will prevail on him to stay more.

"You guys are lucky," this time without the sting. "You didn't go through the hardship and humiliation we went through. In our days, an affair with a white woman was next to impossible, except for those carried on in bars and dance halls. The anti-Filipino feeling was just too strong.

"Marriage was out of the question as it took a state like California, for instance, a long time to decide whether an interracial marriage between, say, a Filipino and an American was legal. It was all right marrying a Mexican, a Puerto Rican or anybody coming from another minority, but not a blonde, blue-eyed American.

"And there was the Watsonville incident. In 1930, the press accused us of taking the women away from the white men, and for being responsible for the venereal diseases in the community. Our barracks were set on fire, resulting in the death of Fermin Tuvera.

"We left the place and vowed never to set foot in Watsonville again. No Filipino went back to this farming town, even long after the perpetrators were punished, and even after the matter was bitterly condemned by both the United States and the Philippines.

"We are told, however, that there is a growing community of Filipinos in Watsonville (California). They must have been there only in recent years, with probably no knowledge of what happened . . . .

"What do you know about Ceferino Garcia?"

"Only as a boxing champion, the second world champion we produced, the first being Pancho Villa."

"Well, more than the boxing champ and bolo-puncher that he was (he now resides in San Diego) Ceferino was a living legend in and out of the ring. When the going was rough for the Pinoys, Ceferino was always there. There was a time when close to 50 armed men swooped down on him, gangland fashion, and you know what? He came out of it unscathed and triumphant."

Stories of this sort are endless. And while a good deal is placed on the negative, they are not for underlining the positive. They are grateful for having been given a chance to work, and to study, even if the last simply meant an exercise in frustration. They are especially grateful for having been allowed to own lands.

Today, scores of Filipino oldtimers work their own farms where once they were hired hands or members of a *padrone* (work-crew made up of five to fifteen laborers. It is from these farms that chayote, saluyot and "baguio" beans are now raised in abundance.)

Today, it is not ususual for a newcomer to bargain with conationals on house rentals. For very likely, the place where he can afford to rent, "for the time being," is that owned by oldtimers who acquired properties from monies kept inside their socks, under their pillows or in belts around their waists. Savings-wise, banks have never attracted them since the Depression.

Corporate talk and stock-market investments are beyond them, They are for investing in real estates, in houses and buildings, in restaurants and things they can see with their own eyes. They will go for condominium ownership only if their partners are of their kind, relatives and townmates. Credit cards have never appealed to them.

Such outlook is reflective of their past. It seems that the years of struggle had had a lasting toll on their lives. They cannot accept the fact, for instance, that the gulf of misunderstanding between themselves and the Americans has already been bridged. That the Watsonvilles are no longer what they used to be. That laws have been repealed. That changes have taken place. That now their children can have the opportunities that once were denied them. Within this framework lies their story.

If they appear different from the farmhands, it is only on the surface. Deep down they are as engaging and out-going. They are especially so when the talk gets around to politics and party alignment. They are die-hard Democrats of the New Deal vintage. Their loyalty to their party can only be superceded by their loyalty to their family.

CHAPTER XI

THE SECOND GENERATION FILIPINOS

Meeting the younger set of Filipinos in America is an experience the new immigrant cannot pass up, not that he wants to. On introduction, they will skip family names lest the same may sound incongruous to such names as Joan, Wilbur, Aaron, Richard, Robert, Mildred and Annette — so it occurs to him.

The doctor, lawyer, nurse, engineer, likewise, makes himself known but unlike in the Philippines where his title rates the kind of response he expects, here he gets a jolt. He is called by his first name. Worse, he is given an American monicker. Dominador becomes Dom, Apolinario Paul, Ruperta Pert instead of Doming, Poling and Pintang.

This is nothing short of manners. The presence of a Filipino professional in their midst hardly makes them uncomfortable. This insouciance towards the just arrived seems to stem from an awareness that they can speak better English. That finishing college is just a matter of time. That compared to their contemporaries back home they are the more fortunate ones. And that actually, there is no difference between the guy who punches electric keys and the guy who plunges sterile needles into epidermis, both of whom owe as much obedience and harbor the same fear to the power complex of the military, business and government, otherwise known as the Establishment.

Whatever the reason may be, he finds them lively and likable enough. "Would they have given us names like Juana, Teopista, Policarpia, Leodegario, Teotimo, Teodulo, Justo or Agapito in the Philippines?"

"That depends—" comes a reply. "With your looks they might have named you Limahong, after a Chinese pirate, or Kerima Putli, after a white, beautiful princess. They might have called you Bulilit, for your size, or Tagong-irit, for your color. Seriously, they might have christened you after a saint. The more common practice is to name a child, especially the first-born, after the father or a favorite relative, usually a grandfather or an uncle, in keeping with the parental spoils system of the country.

"Naming a child after a high-ranking official or after the First Lady becomes a necessity only if there are favors to be asked, like a choice job or a long-overdue raise. Short of this, they will fall back on fancy. Which is to say, naming their wards after boxing champions and celluloid celebrities."

"Tell us, would a study in animal psychology or international agriculture or plant psysiology do us any good in the Philippines?"

"Only if you have in mind working in city zoos — isn't that what the course in animal psychology is for? Or better yet, if you are willing to pull strings. And, only if you are ready to slave it out for P250, or roughly, $35 a month. A course in agronomy could be as frustrating because unless you work your own farm — an activity still frowned on by the *illustrados,* so-called, for their sons — you are likely to deal with absentee landlords and loan sharks."

Explanations of this nature are never really adequate. There are questions and questions and questions. "Is it true that less than 10% of the country's inhabitants own 90% of the land?" That rivers and lakes come handy for sewage disposals?" "That traffic is 50% livestock in the provinces?" "That in Mindanao pearls are given away to those attending a family funeral?" "Do girls and boys date as early as 12 years old?" "Is there excessive fraternization between sexes?" "Is there any serious move towards 'unisex,' the trend which makes it difficult to distinguish boy from girl?"

Exasperating, but then the newly arrived sees through enough that all they want to accomplish with the questioning is to please. More importantly, to reconcile themselves with their origin, and to point out, obliquely, their relevance to America. The second generation Filipinos — offsprings of early settlers, plantation workers and former servicemen (First and Second World Wars) — while retaining fealty for the Philippines and wanting to be identified Filipinos more than possibly Fil-Americans, have no intentions of leaving America. Not for anything. Not for exhortations like *Libre'ng Pilipino!* and *Laging Pilipino!* (Filipino free and always), nor for invocations like "The Philippines is primarily for the Filipinos. Its wealth and natural resources were intended by God for its sons and daughters." (Senator Lorenzo Tanada)

For a fact they do not take offense to epithets like the "uprooted," "transplants," "political hermaphrodites," "lost souls," "*balut* Filipinos," "improvished Americans" because of a knowledge, long held and oftenly stated, that no one in America is American enough, having been migrants at one time, the Red Indians not excluded; that Americans are a minority, whether coming from the long line of English immigrants or Irish, Scot, French, and German stock. They see nothing wrong with being Filipinos away from the Philippines, with being both Filipinos and Americans.

To reinforce this assumption, they ask: "Do you think it would do us any good — or the Philippines — if we leave this place?" "Would a high school diploma, such as most of us have, give us the kind of jobs we want?" "And do you think anyone would be foolish enough to hire us over the hundreds and thousands of unemployed graduates, college graduates in the country today, and for something like $300 or $400 a month?"

"We don't mean to be critical, only reasonable — realistic. Is that being un-Filipino?" "It can even be said that our folks who came here as early as 1903, in sailing schooners, did the old country some good, leaving it instead of remaining in it. The same may be said of you, all of you professionals who are here, don't you think?"

This is the kind of talk the just come hears from the pimply adolescents and young adults when not trying to be amiable. While beauty queens and college orators and whiz kids and pugilists are good things to hear, and to have around, the Filipino or Fil-American youths in America want something more tangible and meaningful to come out of their home country. They want captains of industry, and Nobel prize winners the likes of India's Rabindranath Tagore and Japan's Hideki Yukawa, Schinichiro Tomanaga and Yasunari Kawabata.

They want heros in their midst, as big in life as in death —
Jose Rizal, Andres Bonifacio, Manuel L. Quezon, Jose P. Laurel,
Jose Abad Santos and Claro M. Recto. They want sustained
activities in the arts, started auspiciously in the thirties by Jose
Garcia Villa, then stirred fitfully into existence in the forties and
fifties by Carlos Bulosan, Carlos P. Romulo, N. V. M. Gonzales,
Bienvenido N. Santos, F. Sionil Jose and Nick Joaquin.

For like other ethnic youths in America they too would want
to be proud of their ancestry as much as the society adopting
them. But unlike the Chinese who by training draw heavily from
their rich heritage of art language, shih ching (classic songs)
and their philosophies; the Japanese with their historical ro-
mances, e.g., the noh (skill) drama, the kabuki and bunraku
(puppet) theaters, not to mention their cars, cameras, transistor
radios and wrist watch televisions, the second generation Filipinos find only misgivings of and disgrace for their people.

Imagine, for instance, being told that the Philippines ranks
second in corruption in the world, this from a survey report!

That back home power is very much achieved by manipula-
tion!

That in Honolulu hundreds of their countrymen are seen every
so often being hauled in open police trucks for illegal cockfighting — many of them for the third, fourth, fifth time around!

These are among the things they find difficult to live down,
much less conceal, explain and defend. It seems that to be Filipino must mean being born into a vice, or acquiring one, and
making up for it in church — Sundays. That to be Filipino must
mean apologizing continually for a number of things.

Efforts to keep the young properly informed about their heritage are puny, if non-existent. There are no movements strong enough, or organized and respectable enough to relate, establish and fortify traditions and beliefs. There are only sodality activities — shindigs, outings and gala affairs held in boring regularity.

There is the constant glossing over of little virtues (reconverted jeepneys and tricycles), the endless recitation of the rice terraces "built with no knowledge of engineering 2,000 years ago," the gossamer-like fabric (pina) made by hand in Panay, the long art of the wood-carving — which facts only make the young commiserate: "But why do we have to make things by hand when there are easier ways of doing it?" "Why can't we be more practical and for once less whimsical?"

Obviously, their knowledge of the country is limited to glazed myths and grapevine. While hearing so much of the grandeur of Mayon Volcano in Albay, the stone and steel churches in Manila, the famous bamboo organ in Las Pinas, Rizal, they too must hear about diploma factories, the ineptitude of the entrenched, the bureaucracy of the rich, and about crooks, crooks and crooks.

Nevertheless, the young are as anxious to be Filipinos as Americans. Bonipascio (no typographical error for Bonifacio) Glory, like his sister and eight handsome, hulking brothers in Hawaii, has never been to the Philippines, "but this fact," says he emphatically, "does not make me less a Filipino, ay hindi, po. I'm a Filipino by choice, an American by circumstance, and that's how my kin feel about the whole thing, too."

Lani Altar whose preoccupations include teaching school, editing a newspaper and seeing to it that her children get a regular diet of Philippine culture and history (a nursery child of hers insists on calling Jose Rizal, the country's national hero, Jo-see

Ray-chel) is another Filipino likely to remain as such by duty, preference and responsibility, alongside being American.

Paul Z. Paular, who, like many second generation Filipinos did most of his growing up on a farm before going to college on a GI Bill of Rights, drives it home, thus: "Make no mistake about it — I'm too Filipino to the point of being anti-American, especially on matters where the Philippines is concerned." (This, despite an unhappy incident with a Philippine customs official who told him flush on the face the last time he was home, that he was no longer a Filipino. "You should know that. Your passport clearly indicates your citizenship.")

A good number of second generation Filipinos feel that strong about the Philippnes to pass for racists and raving radicals. They are for committing to heart Rizal's *Noli Me Tangere*, for quoting passages from Manuel Boaken's book, "I Lived With the American People," which recalls in crackling prose the strife of the Filipinos in America before the days of Bataan and Corregidor.

They are for letting their children (third generation) attend Philippine summer schools (see appendix), for letting them learn Pilipino, sing native songs. They are for trundling off their wards, Chinese-like, to the old country, "there to study and imbibe the spirit of the race." They are for joining councils and for organizing clubs. For just about anything to keep the fires of Filipinism alive in themselves.

CHAPTER XII

THE NAVY GUYS

There is another breed of Filipinos the immigrant is likely to encounter sooner than he expects because besides their number, 20,000 strong in the West Coast area alone, they are seen in obvious places making up for much of the realities deferred at sea. If they are not clicking away at polaroid cameras they are licking at stamps for those postcards and letters that must be sent home. They are for ridding themselves of greenbucks by the fistful. Who said about Ilocanos being parsimonious?

The Ilocanos who constitute 85% of the Filipinos in the United States Navy, Marine Corps and Coast Guard are responsible for many of those beer joint and dress-up affairs. They are for spending money on a countryman, for insisting on getting together "again, in a week's time, or the next," depending on how they can make out in crap games.

Seat of activity is generally the naval city of San Diego where most of them are based. They invade Los Angeles, San Francisco and other cities nearby for much the same reason, although for a more valid one, they go to such places to shop around for dates among the newly arrived, just in case.

Unlike the oldtimers who must face outright rejection, because of age, the navy guys have better chances of winning a nurse, teacher or doctor. Age gap is not as conspicuous. In fact, with junior officers a Filipina is reduced overnight into a veronica. She does not waste time at quibbling, concealed modesty or un-attended silence. She whoops it up first-class: wedding, reception and all.

The rage for the navy species vary accordingly. Sergeants of sorts who like being identified as petty officers are given just enough of the usual run-around. They are made to go through weeks of homage, Philippine-style, akin to "hewing wood and drawing water," before they are taken seriously. When accepted they are made to wait for one or two years.

The reason: brothers and sisters must still have to be helped through college; the old folks must have to be provided for in old age. Once such obligations are met, reasonably, a not too-elaborate wedding is drawn up, and why should it be otherwise? Isn't the nurse, teacher or doctor, who holds two or three jobs and therefore in a better financial position, picking the tab for both the ritual and the reception?

The seamen with no brass or chevrons to speak of are not too keenly welcome in visiting parlors, even with the bars of candy and the boxes of canned goods they give away. But somehow half of them who try manage to come through. They get them-selves a nurse or a prize jewel of a doctor. When this happens there is jubilation and sadness compounded — for the bride who must look at the happenstance as an arrangement; for the bridegroom who must regard the whole affair as a windfall. The bride whose visa, to begin with, was dubious can now hope to remain permanently on the strength of a navy husband. The latter can now expect to finish school and take things easy without having to look for odd jobs once muzzled out of service.

It is an unflattering situation to be in for the truly idealist, but who among the Filipinos in Amerca can claim idealism of the kind? The nurse, teacher, doctor who came as immigrant, or who did come undercover, compromised or gave up completely such big little traits as patroitism, selflessness, social responsibility, and even love of home and country. More so with the navy guys who on entering the service are made to swear and sign papers to that effect, and who upon nearing completion of prescribed duty actively, if ostensibly, seek naturalization. Attaining Amercan citizenship is to them, after all, a mark of achievement.

Their rationale runs all the way from fact to fiction, hearsay to heresy, ill feelings to noble intentions. One serviceman puts it thus: "I would never have made it in the Philippines. You see, I come from a god-forsaken family and an equally god-forsaken barrio. If I go back, I'd be where I had left off, working myself to the bone in somebody else's farm, not getting anywhere. I'd be a sure prey to loan sharks and those other smart guys in town. Or, maybe with my little knowledge of automotive I'd be a chauffeur-mechanic-utility man to some filthy rich family — if by then, I've not taken to the hills, clearly a fugitive of some sort."

Another has this to say: "You see, *choy, hanap buhay lang ito.* (I'm here only to make a living.) Once I get hold of the bag,

I'll pack up and head straight for home. I will probably start a business of my own. I will employ as many of my idle townmates. That way I could not be accused of having turned my back to the land of my birth. I would not as you would say, have to contend with a conscience."

Still another: "I'd like to see the old country again, and who wouldn't? But for the present I'm for putting it off. I hear so much about pockets being picked clean under one's nose, and people molested even in broad daylight. To make matters worse, why are storms and earthquakes and droughts more frequent now than it used to be?"

And another: "What, back to the Philippines? No, thank you. I don't think I failed her, she failed me . . . I'm a hundred times better off here. I've my own car, my own color television set, my own movie camera. Do you think I would have acquired all these in the space of two years, on a soldier's pay back home? Let me put it this way: I've come to like this place. America is my present; the Philippines, my past."

The consensus among the Filipinos in the Navy is not for going home, except for visits or for such emergencies as attending a mother's or father's funeral. They are for staying in America, for becoming naturalized Americans. "There are no jobs for us there, not the kind we want, anyway. There is no piece of property for us to inherit, and nothing to draw us back really."

As if discovering an ally in the doctor, nurse and engineer they then ask: "Isn't that the same with you, too? That things have become difficult even for those finishing four-year courses in college?"

"Six to nine years," says the doctor.

"OK, six to nine years. Isn't that a disgrace that you too must come here like us?"

He smiles, and taking this to mean approval more than simple acknowledgement they go off again. They hit the mulcters, the New Rich, the inept, the affluent and the powerful, ending each line or statement with *hinda ba, pare?* (Isn't that so?)

Actually these furious denunciations are nothing but feeble mouthings to cover up for a step they are about to take: that is, renounce old allegiance for new, to become American citizens while still in the service or within the six-month period after their termination of duty. If it can be helped, they want to be Filipinos as much as Americans, to be part of the Philippine constituency, even in the knowledge that the same is no longer possible physically and legally. They would want to be part of the "dream and the destiny," whatever meanings that may hold for them, to be counted on on both sides, to be able to say either way with just as much pride, "Yes, we are Filipinos," or "Yes, we are Americans."

For having gone through a war in Vietnam and elsewhere, they feel that they are entitled to a little privilege: namely, to be Americans at certain times, Filipinos at other times. They want to be accepted as Americans in America, Filipinos when in the Philippines or when in the company of Filipinos or Fil-Americans.

This is neither ironical nor anomalous. The Filipino navy men, while thinking American in may ways will continue to be Filipinos. They will do things Filipino more than they would American, for all their rejection of the old country and their passion for the new. While "digging" the American idiom, they will persist at every possible chance on speaking Pilipino or any of their own dialects. Sentiments will run deep just as much as it will prevail upon reality.

They will crave for native delicacies — *turon, ginataan* and *bibingka*. They will be homesick for *santacruzan* (May processions) and town fiestas, the warmth of old friends and relatives, and lazy evenings around market stalls. They will seek their countryman, or ex-countryman, spend good money on him. They will choose a Filipina nurse, teacher or doctor for a wife more than they would a non-Filipina.

They will bring up their children in the tradition of the old country. There will be kissing of hands, polite conversations and restrained silences at mealtime. The father will lord it over, firmly laying down the rules of conduct and exhorting his wards with homilies. The mother will accept her second-class role of absorber, reminder and crossbearer, equal rights amendment for women notwithstanding and notwithstanding the fact that she earns twice or thrice as much as the master of the house. The whole family will kneel down before a candle-lighted icon before repairing to bed.

All these genuflections to things Philippines and adherence to native ways are all right — pardonable and understandable — so notes the Filipino professional, if the relationship between the Philippines and America remains on an even keel, if military and economic commitments on the part of the latter continue to hold sway. In the event of change or modification of policies which may arise as a result of geopolitics or differences in national and international objectives, the Filipino navy men, now naturalized or almost so, would be in a most unhappy position.

"When that happens, what?" quips a doctor. "Where would you be? Which side will you take?"

"Exactly where you will be, Doc."

Short of such an exigency, the loyalty of the Filipino navy men will continue to be dual: one seemingly secret, the other obviously open. They will be as much for America as for the Philippines, and vice-versa. They will continue to be star-spangled Filipinos, or more properly "greenhorn" Americans, whether living in simplicity or raging in diversity.

CHAPTER XIII

THE HYPHENATES

In the Philippines the mestizos and mestizas (those who trace their ancestry to Spanish grandees and some other foreigners) are a fortunate breed. They own wide tracts of lands, and are entrenched in corporate positions. They get the best of seats, the choicest of harvests, and a following that is almost subservient.

They naturally have no complaints to make, except perhaps the surge of student unrest, which today is partly directed against them, not because of hybridism but because of advantages gained for being hybrids.

Between a Filipino-Filipino and a Spanish-Filipino or American-Filipino, the latter is likely to win out, e.i., get the better employment where glamor, if looks and build, family origin and conditions surrounding their birth are the main, though unwritten, considerations. They "lord" it over in airlines, banks, movies, milti-million-peso bottling companies and other giant industries.

Identity, generally a problem with offsprings of mixed parentage involving a minority, is not a problem with them, because to begin with they have been made to believe that they are the real thing.

This is not quite the case with the Filipino hyphenates in the United States, those who by blood are American-Filipino, German-Filipino, Irish-Filipino, Mexican-Filipino, Portuguese-Filipino, Hawaiian-Filipino, African-Filipino, Spanish-Filipino, Russian-Filipino, Guamenian-Filipino, Aluet-Filipino or Indian-Filipino.

In America the Philippine mestizos and mestizas are somewhat of a displaced group, straining for recognition and dignity both within the small circle to which they are thrown in (the Filipino community or the other communities to which their other self must find validity) and the larger circle (the American scene) to which they would ultimately like to belong.

For a choice they would have much preferred being brown or black or red or yellow or white to being half and half something. "At least with just one shade," says an Irish-Filipino, "I'd know where I'd be, where I could gain acceptance without trying very hard — really. As it is I have to apologize and explain a lot.

"I have to excel in two or three cultures, that of my father's, my mother's and the larger society's. Which is tough, if you know what I mean. You have to contend with so much cynicism and prejudice.

"Just making it is not enough. You have to be the best. The

strongest and slyest of quarterbacks. A holder of a Ph.D. (a master's would sound like a college drop-out) and a guy with some promise of making a million bucks. Otherwise, you are not that successful German, Filipino or American."

Says a Russian-Filipino: "One's loyalty to anything is never really taken at face value. I suppose this is natural. People will always look with doubt on one not completely belonging to his kind. For instance, I cannot get into a room of brown-skinned men and women without causing eyebrows to be raised in disbelief and/or distrust, without making me self-conscious and embarrassed. I get the same feeling in a gathering of white people."

Indeed, for all their improved, if dominant features, the Philippine mestizos and mestizas in America seem to lack the confidence which their counterparts back home are full of. Instead of wanting to lead they find it more convenient to follow. They do not feel beholden. On the contrary, they feel suspect and slightly out of place.

Alfred Mendoza, a Fil-American himself, in his pilot study of the mestizo element in America, writes: "Attitudes seem to support that physical features play a significant role in the identification process and experience. Where the features are strongly stereotypical, identification is taken for granted . . . Where the features place the individual in a position of marginality, the frequent questioning he encounters serve as constant reminder of his position. He becomes more attuned and sensitive to the aspects of race and the attitudes of others."

If it can be helped they are for keeping their silence on matters of pedigrees and background. Such things, they point out, are not good for the psyche and therefore serve no gainful purpose. It only succeeds in splintering up an already splintered group.

But every now and then a girl like Joy Atienza (an assumed name) comes up and "tells it like it is:" "I'm what you may call an undesirable product of an undesirable union. My parents were ashamed of each other, Father being Brown and Mother being White. Their marriage was never sanctioned, legally and socially.

"But let me tell you, inside our house we were a great family. We laughed a lot. We talked a good deal about everything. Things, however, became different the moment we stepped out, for a walk in the park or for a shopping trip.

"Father never walked beside us. He was always either ahead of us or behind us. Mother tried filling me up on Father's strange behavior, but somehow this did not help. I could not understand, for instance, why Mother's friends and family were not necessarily Father's, why, in restaurants, Father ate his sandwich outside standing up, while Mother and I sat out in a corner, nibbling a hamburger — a bowl of salad staring us in the eye.

"I grew up, as most of my kind did, in this atmosphere, with Father and Mother eventually breaking up. They broke up, I think, not so much because of themselves but because of the society they lived in.

"But let me say this, my childhood was not that bad. At least with me, I knew the meaning of having a mother, even for just a brief period of time. With many of my Filipino-American contemporaries, they grew up not knowing the likes of one."

It was like this before the fifties. Interracial marriages were scoffed at and to some extent tabooed. Nevertheless the brown man and the white woman went ahead. Unions after unions came about just as separations and divorces followed.

Caught in the confusion were the children. But the Filipino father, instead of committing his wards to foster homes, took the matter upon himself. He raised them up the best way he knew how, in the culture of his race.

So it is that while looking more American than Filipino, the mestizos and mestizas feel more Filipinos than Americans. They are rice-eaters instead of flour-consumers, Catholics instead of Protestants. They are at home with Filipinos more than they are with Americans.

They will join Filipino groups more than they would other communities, despite awareness of extravagance and misdirection of affairs. Shirley Rivera, a Red Indian-Filipino will not mind spending good money to see herself proclaimed Miss Philippines in the Los Angeles area; neither would Diane Giles, a Black-Filipino, who was Miss Filipino Community of San Francisco for a Fourth of July festivities.

It is no idle wish on the part of the mestizos to see an American bred Filipino becoming president of the Philippines in the tradition of Eamon de Valera, a New York-born (1882 -   ) Irish-American who for years since 1918 was either President or taoiseach of the Republic of Ireland.

This desire to belong and to excel in their group is native with the older Filipino-Americans, those born in less happier conditions, before the fifties. With the more recent vintage of Filipino-Americans, they are for wanting to belong and to achieve prominence not in the country of their father, but in their own.

"It's different with me. It has to be," says a high school student emphatically. "Father is Filipino. I am American. I feel that way about the whole thing."

This attitude has became increasingly inevitable with the very young. In the last twenty years, corrective legislations and Supreme Court rulings on miscegenation have brought about sweeping changes in this respect. As a result, the Brown man is no longer ashamed to walk with a White woman, and vice-versa. Children are now brought up differently, if normally, without the parents parting ways to give in to the harsh demands of society.

In California, history books are undergoing face-lifting to include Filipinos and other Asians who have distinguished themselves in the social, political and economic life of the state and nation. The philosophy behind such move is not to make the Filipino-Americans more Filipinos than Americans, but as proud Americans coming from a stock as much like as any, and possibly as much sought after. This seems to work out fine. For today, sure of their footings, the Philippine hyphenates among the very young are well on the way to getting up there — big, as never before.

CHAPTER XIV

THE FIRST BATCH OF PROFESSIONALS

One set of people the newcomer is most likely to have dealings with are conationals of his who served as civilian employees in Guam. Like him, they too are doctors, dentists, accountants, architects and engineers; contemporaries or just about, and as much inclined to the hard virtues and easy vices of the homeland.

They had planned to work in Guam for only three years, the length of time they were under contract, but the McCarran-Walter Act in 1952, vesting the Attorney General and his subordinates discretionary powers as to who can remain or who can be admitted permanently on the basis of qualitative selection, changed all that. They came to the mainland instead, to work and save some more.

And worked and saved they did. More: they made their presence felt by their efforts at excellence and achievement. They became office managers, bank executives, personnel heads, construction engineers, senior accountants, travel agents, restaurateurs, organizers of local development programs, and active members of Optimist, Lion and Jaycee clubs.

But like all else they did not spring full-blown in the land. The hundreds and thousands who came from this island-base had to wear off their shoes before landing a job. An engineer describes the process, thus: "I do not know how many times I filled out application forms, submitted resumes and appeared for interviews. But always, I was told the same thing: there was nothing for me. Nothing. My college background and three-year work experience in Guam were of little help.

"On my fifth or sixth month, I was ready to climb walls. I was prepared to quit — to go home. But where was I to get transportation money? I had by then burned up my savings. I was subsisting on raw carrots. There were even times when I had to skip meals because I could not afford the stuff. The nearest Pinoy was always some blocks away, or something like one or two hours 'journey' on foot. Many of our countrymen were in Bakersfield, Modesto, Salinas, Stockton, Portland, Seattle, Santa Barbara, San Luis Obispo, San Ramon and all the Sans and Santas along the Pacific coast — places that were prohibitive for guys like us without transportation. It took us years to have cars of our own, because to begin with, it took that long to land good jobs."

"Was the employment climate that bad?"

"No."

"What took that long then?"

"Circumstances, I suppose. Having known the Filipinos as mere farmhands, domestic helps or restaurant fixtures — a matter not entirely our own doing — the Americans could not imagine us suddenly teaching school, disbursing monies, directing construction projects, comforting the afflicted, and taking over their affairs. It simply was unbelievable.

"To prove them wrong, however, we had to work a little extra. We had to push a little more. Which meant, for most of us from Guam, going back to school and passing licensure examinations on fast dwindling finances.

"It was tough weathering prejudice, and making the Americans realize that we too could be part of Establishment. I do not know whether we are making any grounds on this, but I do know we are not relaxing our efforts towards that end."

That seems easy to tell. Today, the immigrant-Filipino of the fifties make home in the West and East Coasts, with relatively small number migrating to the Middle and Southern States. They have married into the ranks of Filipino nurses (former exchange students and recent arrivals), teachers, dentists, doctors and pharmacists.

The late Conrado Salumbides, a braintrust of the Guamenian group, was as much listened to on subjects about Philippine affairs as he was on matters concerning conglomerates, being a public certified accountant and a key man to a giant computer organization in California.

Victor Zapanta, a civil engineer, has a camp following by the hundreds, having led a Croesus life in Guam for fortunes made in stevedoring. (The Filipinos in this U.S. territory were divided sharply into two groups: those from the Visayan islands stayed in Camp Roxas, so named after the first President of the Philippine Republic, Manuel Roxas, a favorite son of the Visayas; those from Northern Luzon stayed in Camp Quezon, so named after Commonwealth President Manuel L. Quezon. Zapanta served, as he still does, as a catalyst to these factions in his capacity as acknowledged leader, great friend and philantrophist of sorts.)

Zosimo O. Majuelo, one of the few who married a Filipina in Guam (the ratio of Philippine male and female in the place at the time was 150 to one), now runs a bustling travel agency in the heart of Los Angeles, together with his wife, Salud. Like him, she is au courant on air travel. She explains, for instance, that a straight line, while the shortest distance between two points, is not necessarily the cheapest when taking a plane. "A passenger can fly from Phoenix to Los Angeles to San Francisco for less than it would cost to fly direct from Phoenix to San Francisco. The trick is in knowing such matters as intrastate commuter fare."

Victor Bernardo has a posh restaurant in Burbank, the nation's present studio capital. With homeland motif, soft music, Oriental cuisines and personal charm, his place has attracted wide patronage of the Anthony Quinn, Rock Hudson and Sylva Koscina variety.

Zoilo Inacay is another Guamenian Filipino who has gone a long way from obscurity to prominence. Besides rating a monthly income of four digits, he heads one of the more prestigious organizations in San Francisco, the Filipino Professionals and

Businessmen's Association, which counts on such distinguished members as Cesar Ortiz, Marcelo Eclevia, Gerry Sy, Dr. Ernesto Hilario, Dr. Amancio Ergina, Ronald Cacas, A. Marquez Bautista, Dr. Apolonio R. Dimapilis, Jack Bautista, Jimmy Jacinto, Or. Vincent D. Quita, Jose de los Reyes, Ricardo S. Morada, Manuel Nery, Fernando L. Zulueta, Demetrio S. Jayme, Antonio M. Orbeta, Ronnie C. Avenida, Drs. Adolfo Badillo, Ben Candelaria, Rodolfo S. Duterte, Mario Borja, Carlos V. Garcia, Fernando G. Gomez, Manuel Luna, Leonilo Malabed, Alfonso Ver, G. B. Policar and others.

Johnny Carandang, like Salumbides, Majuelo and Zapanta, has headed a "white man's club." As president of the Evening Optimist Club of Downtown Los Angeles, he has raised its membership to class A category, won for himself and the Club seven major awards, including an international trophy of excellence for community service and the Best Club of the Year Award (1970) in the Southwest Pacific area. In winning the last award, Lt. Governor James E. Attarian writes, in part: "John, I personally want you to know that I am aware that your ability as a leader was one of the reasons for it all. Your club must really think much of you and hold you in high esteem to have put out the amount of work that they did. With those three ingredients, ability, work and esteem for each other as well as yourself, the result was inevitable."

Alfonso Sauz, Doming Langit, Rudy Lontok, Pete Dizon, Rey Velez, Dr. Jose Pascual, Dem Hechanova, Mike Carillo, Dr. Manuel Fajardo, Leo Eriman, Jose Ros, Valerio Reyes, all of whom making a stint in Guam before coming to the mainland, are today names in the social register. Their ability for socializing is over-shadowed only by their intensity, if talent, in their own work.

As a result of this thrust to prominence, the Filipinos are no longer consigned statistically and publicly to the category of "Orientals and others" or "Indians and others" or "people with Spanish surnames." In the 1970 census, the Filipinos seemed to have arrived on a status identity of their own. (Quint Villanueva, a Filipino by extraction, is to be given some credit. While negotiating for his candidacy for state congress, he had a direct hand in putting a stop to the "and others" or "people with Spanish surnames" classification of Filipinos.)

Today, there is a demand for Filipinos, seemingly, in the professional level, including those finishing in Los Banos and Munoz agricultural schools. The need for agricultural graduates to work in technical, managerial and skilled occupations was felt as early as the sixties. Talks were initiated in the higher councils of government between the United States of America and the Republic of the Philippines.

As a result, close to 2,000 college trained and specialized workers were recruited from the Philippines. On a go-ahead signal from then Secretary of Labor Norberto Romualdez, Jr., planes from the Philippine Air Lines, the nation's flag carrier, were chartered, and for weeks, in 1963, Labor Technical Assistant Joaquin Tiong was never a busier man. He accompanied the farm experts to Yuma, Arizona and to such other farm towns in the West, where for two years they dutifully fulfilled their contractual obligations, before transferring to hospital projects, research centers, and curiously to banks where remuneration was more attractive and working conditions less stringent.

Like the Filipinos coming from Guam, the farm experts chose to remain in America, and did so on a permanent term. Proper offices were sought with little difficulty. The 2,000 or so skilled and technical help from the Philippines were among the 23,000 immigrant workers certified by the U.S. Department of Labor to the Departments of Justice and State in 1965. Not one of the 2,000-odd has gone home to roost, for home to them has become, expectedly, the United States of America. They have gone back only as tourists or for emergencies in the family.

The picture created by the first batch of professionals in the 1950s and those immediately following has been impressive and far-reaching. It did much in opening the floodgates for the Philippine professionals. It did help in eliminating the national-origins of quota allocation, the old basis of immigration assignment, as it did in erasing the irrational concept of ethnic superiority in the immigration laws of the United States.

Today, there are more Filipinos employed in banks, than there are other nationalities, except Canadians, English and Americans. A typical example is the California Federal Bank. In its October 1970 assessment, its staff had the following aliens: Argentina - 1, Australia- 1, Austria - 3, Belgium - 1, Canada - 25, China - 2, Columbia - 1, Cuba - 4, Czechoslovakia - 1, England - 12, Estonia - 1, France - 2, Germany - 10, Greece - 1, Holland - 1, Hong Kong - 2, Hungary - 1, India - 1, Indonesia - 2, Iran - 1, Ireland - 4, Italy - 1, Japan - 2, Korea - 2, Lithuania - 1, Malta - 1, Mexico - 3, Norway - 1, Panama - 2, Philippines - 11, Poland - 1, Samoa - 1, Scotland - 2, South Africa - 1, Turkey - 2, Wales - 1, and Yugoslavia - 2. They are in various departments from accounting and advertising to legal and loan service to escrow and engineering.

Not-too-surprisingly, the line of questioning has shifted from "What country are you from?" to "What can you do?" Lately, there seems to be no need for that kind of query. For more than

just numbers (31,203 immigrants in 1970, the biggest number
from an Asian nation at any one time) the Filipinos have made
themselves patent: they will preempt positions, shoot high —
even when not challenged.

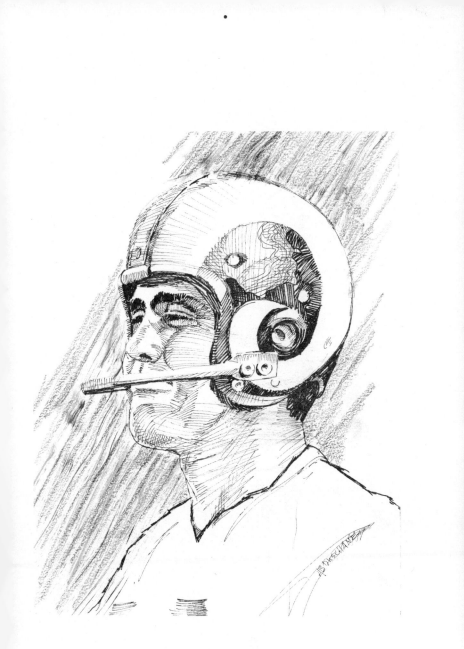

Ram's Quarterback Roman Gabriel, 6' 4" and 220 lbs., is the biggest Filipino contribution in athletics.

Political relevance is ach
by Filipinos in Los Angeles through the leadership of Dr

Villaflor, above receiving a recognition plaque from Mayor
Yorty before leaders in the community.

Romy Madrigal (left) rose from the ranks and is now plant
superintendent of a giant canning factory in Southern California.
James Misahon is shown addressing the Governor's Conference
on Immigration (Hawaii) of which he was chairman.

Pomping Vila is top-notch organist, shown above with wife, Tanya, an opera singer. Right, Lalaine Bennett (Mrs. Felix Skievaski), a Miss Philippines Universe runner-up, rears a family in suburban Federal Way, Washington.

Health Day in Los Angeles, headed by Dr. Jenny Batongmalaque, placed Filipinos in focus; below, summer schools are afforded children of Philippine parentage.

Johnny Carandang's activities in Optimism puts Filipino Optimist Club in perspective. He is shown receiving an award, one of many he got, from International president Monroe Marlowe. Right, The Society of Seven is one of the highest paid combos in the country.

Dr. Mario Pamatmat, shown in his office at the University of Washington, is an authority on seabeds; Gerardo Casuga, right, is one of the more successful Filipino farmers, who at 65 still takes care of acres of orange trees in Orange Cove, Sunkist capital of the world.

The Filipino "muscles" in key areas are provided by Congressman Oliver Lunasco and Municipal Judge Maria Lacadia Obera.

PART THREE

RISE IN STATUS

CHAPTER XV

A FOOT ON THE LADDER

Although the Filipinos have yet to produce authentic contributions in the nature of Italy's Toscanini, Amadeo P. Giannini and Joe DiMaggio or Japan's Daniel Inoye and S. I. Hayakawa, the promise is quite evident. They have gone over impressively in art, music, education, medicine, science, government and other fields of endeavor.

In painting, the Filipino is the "sensitive," "versatile" and "highly-gifted" artisan. When he came, has was a bundle of compromises, awkward and unsure. Today, he has gained acceptance and respectability. He has picked up awards in San Francisco, Monterey and Los Angeles. He is — for purposes — Arthur Duchane, Buddy Reyes, Cesar Amorsolo, Bobby Portillo, Sylvestre P. Mateo, Mary McIntosh, Alfred Robles, Jose Duchane, Carlos Villa, Manansala, Tinsay, Jesse P. Santos and Ben Inocencio.

He has even gone to teach school. Leo Vallador is an instructor at San Francisco Art Institute, so is Joaquin Legaspi at San Francisco State College. Val M. Laigo is assistant professor of art at Seattle University. In a class by himself is Corky Trinidad whose cartoons are front page stuffs in Honolulu and whose works are syndicated in 20 newspapers in the mainland, the *Los Angeles Times* included.

In the allied arts the Filipino is just as remarkable. Ambrosio D. Molo is an awardee for penmanship mastery; Inocencio Padua for outstanding contributions in photography. Ignacio M. Sarmiento is an Emmy recipient for coproduction done on "Adoption — Ben Hunter Matinee." Isagani Pastor is a standout in film work. Apart from being an award-winning editor, he is a cinematographer and director par excellence. George Sunga, of Smother Brothers and Tom Jones' fame, is another Filipino who has made notable strides in television. But, as it is in the game, stars Leon Lontok, Barbara Luna, Nelly Adams, Anakorita (Helen Thompson) and Conrad Parham are more well known.

The nightclub type of entertainment is, however, almost like a Philippine concession. Whether beating the drums, playing the piano, strumming a guitar, singing, dancing or mimicking, the Filipino is the thing. The Family Tree commands top billing anywhere. The Reycards (Reynaldo Ramirez and Ricardo Castro) are a rage in Las Vegas, Lake Tahoe, Los Angeles and Hawaii. The Montecillo Sisters are a bargain, and half a dozen other combos (Rene Paulo Quartet, Sun Spots, Manila Machine, Oriental Blend, Moses and the Highbrows and the Paulets) are a smash. The Society of Seven has achieved the sophistication of the truly elite, with earnings like $25,000 a week.

On the basis of individual performances the ones that come

to mind readily are Evelyn Mandac, Linda Andal, Joe Foz and Pomping Vila. Vila holds court nightly to a clientele in Pasadena where he performs on a six-tiered organ in the tradition of a maestro. Joe Foz attracts nightclub *aficionados* from all over Southern California for his piano-playing in San Diego. Andal, on the other hand, sings in New York where she is great shakes. Mandac, a lyric soprano, also campaigns in the Big Town where she gets rave notes of importance.

The roster of Filipinos in education is substantial enough to impress archivists. The bigger-than-life-figures include Dr. Dulzura Villaflor, Dr. Manuel S. Rustia, Domingo Los Banos, James J. M. Misahon, the Toralballas, Msgr. Osmundo Calip, Julita T. Mcleod, Precioso M. Nicanor, Virginia Sta. Maria, Dr. Anastacio L. Palafox, Dr. Telesforo Luna, Mrs. Clay Ignacio, Fely Cordero, Dr. Maxima Dandoy, Dr. Albert Bacdayan, Wilfredo Al. Clemente, Dr. Sofia L. Prudenciano and Jose Bonpua, Jr.

Besides teaching college and heading the Federation of Philippine Teachers in U. S., Bonpua writes penetrating articles on Philippine affairs. Dr. Prudenciano is the female Horatio Alger. Starting as a gradeschool teacher, she has risen to graduate school professorship in a span of ten years.

Clemente is author and political scientist (Wisconsin State University). Dr. Bacdayan, a Ford Foundation grantee, is professor of anthropology at Western Kentucky University. Dr. Dandoy is with Fresno State College as professor of social studies. Cordero is with Harbor College and Los Angeles City College, and is author of a book on sociology. Mrs. Ignacio teaches foreign languages at the University of Washington. Dr. Luna is geography professor in Hawaii. Also at the University of Hawaii is Dr. Palafox who, besides teaching poultry science, is responsible for 48 scientific publications on the subject.

Sta. Maria's credentials are as follows: educator-counselor of the San Francisco Unified School District, co-founder and president of the Fil-Am Teachers Association; Nicanor's: author, journalist, professional lecturer on book publication, recipient of the mayoral (New York) citation for cultural contributions. Mcleod's: principal, Washington Irving Elementary School; instructor, San Francisco State College Summer Program; member, advisory board, Philippine Studies, San Francisco State College; organizer of Maligaya Dance Troupe, and voted one of the "Ten Most Outstanding Women of 1969" by the *San Francisco Examiner*.

Divinity Professor Msgr. Calip (St. John, Notre Dame, Michigan State University and the University of San Francisco) is the spiritual fountainhead of the Catholic Filipinos in America. The Toralballas (Leopoldo and Gloria) are of the Einstein mold. Gloria is a doctoral fellow and research for the Office of Scientific Research. On the sides, she teaches chemistry at Hunter College, Columbia and Marquette. Leopoldo is mathematics professor, New York University.

In Hawaii, the big man in education is Misahon. He is administrative director, Office of the Vice President for Continuing Education and Community Service, University of Hawaii. In 1969, he was chairman of the Governor's Statewide Conference on Immigration in Hawaii, which helped solve unemployment and the harsh administrative procedures and processing of immigrants. The other big man is Los Banos. Before becoming assistant superintendent of public schools, Los Banos was the official mentor of the Cambodian royal family, in addition to being coach of the Cambodian basketball team which saw action in the Rome Olympics.

With Dr. Rustia, the years go back to the University of the Philippines where he was dean of a college, adviser to Presidents, and authority on tariff policies and the Chinese role in Philippine economy. He was top echelon for Boeing before going back to teaching (University of Washington), for what he calls "a sentimental journey." He is 71 and the intellectual leader of the Filipinos in Seattle.

Dr. Villaflor heads the nexus of Philippine organizations in Los Angeles. As such, she is regarded matriarch cum laude by a good number of kababayan. Her credentials on education and involvement in Philippine affairs are arm-long.

It is in medicine, however, that the Filipino name is legion. In Chicago alone, there are more than 500 physicians and surgeons who are outstanding in their own right. They have passed the crucible of public acceptance, and are the myth-builders of Philippine image. The names of Agana, Atol, Acasio, Balagot, Battung, Botuyan, Baguindoc, Bayona, Buquiran, Calub, Casaclang, Dacanay, Dumlao, Dumpit, Gaffud, Gabuya, Ladlad, Limpin, Magno, Maglaya, Macaladad, Pangilinan, Palu-ay, Reotutar, Saclolo, Orig, Yadao, Yanong and Zagala, while foreign-sounding, are no longer strange in the medical world.

There is, in fact, a Filipino doctor anywhere in America. In Maui, where the props of Heaven are still intact, Jose L. Romero goes about his way attending to the health needs of 48,000 inhabitants (1,400 of whom are Filipinos), advising married adults to have sex daily "in order to strengthen the muscles of the heart." In Honolulu, the doctor is either Fely Bunao-Ylarde, Mario Bautista, Henry Manayan, Cora Manayan or Cesar de

Jesus; in Long Beach, Antonio Lozada or Iluminada Martin; in Monrovia, Pilar Centeno.

Prominence has come to Jesus C. Bacala, of Kentucky, for books written on nursing; to Ted Ulanday, of Santa Clara, for achievement on eye practice; to the Umalis (Filemon and Elias), of Virginia and Washington D.C., respectively, for obstetrics and gynecology; to Ricardo J. Crudo, of New York, for professional services beyond the realm of duty; to Mariano Madarang Rayos, for teaching interns and residents at St. Luke's, Children's Hospital and St. Mary's Medical Center in San Francisco.

In Los Angeles, the top crusts are Jenny Batongmalaque, Epifanio Espinas, Roland Navarro and Bienvenido Tan. Tan parlayed a modest savings on hospitals and is now considered the most successful, financially. Navarro did, as he still does, miracles on heart patients and is well on the way to becoming a Laennec, French doctor-inventor of the stethoscope, who is said to know the condition of a patient even while "standing well away from the sickbed." Espinas, on the other hand, is a "Who's Who" for feats done on open heart surgery, while Batongmalaque is a "Who's Who" candidate for singular achievements on the Filipino Health day (July 11, 1971), in which 200 volunteers, professionals and non- professionals alike, gave all-out support to assist her in servicing the health and community needs of more than 2,000 Filipinos and non-Filipinos. (A book on the project is underway.)

Bold steps are also being undertaken elsewhere. Angelo Ozoa is starting a health plan in Los Gatos, California where he is medical director of Sunlight Valley Hospital. Luis Advincula has health programs going in Greencastle, Indiana where he is also a medical director.

The workers, however, who have given, more to the effort of image- building are the nurses. They constitute the biggest group of Filipino professionals in America. But density is not what makes them truly noteworthy. Besides efficiency, they have shown qualities of endurance, disposition and intelligence, which have placed them in great demand in any branch of nursing service. Bertha Sanchez may well be the epitome of the Filipino nurse. Selected one of the "Ten Most Outstanding Women of 1969" by the *San Francisco Chronicle*, she holds the coveted position of International Director of Project Concern in Vietnam.

In the world of science, breakthroughs have been made by Rolando Luna, Luis Azarraga, Mauro A. Medina, Pedro Paloma and Dr. Mario Pamatmat. Pamatmat, a research-scientist of the University of Washington, has made strides in measuring the oxygen consumption of life under the seas. He has gone to the bottom of oceans to establish the commercial possibility of fluvial agriculture. Paloma, of Scripps Institute, is another oceanographer who studies seabeds in order to determine the carbon cycle of organisms. Medina, a first-rate methematician, is indispensable for an international telecommunication company. Azarraga has made the Little Red Book in Science with his "camerama," a breadbasket camera that can take more than six miles of panoramic skyline. Rolando Luna is an engineer-scientist of the Advance Space Systems Division which worked on Logistics Craft, Manned Orbital Research Laboratory, Apollo Space Vehicle and the Mars-bound Voyagers.

In the more glamorous field of government, the Filipinos have likewise risen to importance and distinction. Maria Lacadia Obrera is a municipal judge in Los Angeles; Glenn Olea is a councilmen in Seaside; Victor Agmata is a prosecuting attorney in Hawaii; Oliver Lunasco is a state representative of Oahu, Hawaii; Oscar Delfin is a state senator of Guam. Benjamin Menor, a former state representative, is a circuit judge in Hawaii; Barney Menor and Pedro de la Cruz were twice state representatives of Oahu and Maui-Molokai, respectively. Bernardo Bicoy, Peter Aduja and Emilio Alcon were also state representatives in Hawaii.

In sports, three names make the most sense: Cecile Martinez who is ranked 8th nationally in women's tennis; Mitchell Palacio who is a 15-year old national judo champion (Junior Division), youngest Judoka to be presented the degree of Shodan (first degree black belt) and winner of 150 trophies and medals; Superstar Quarterback Roman Gabriel who is a household word, and a great source of pride of every Filipino in America.

In the communication media, Ernesto Flores, Cipriano Ayalin, Rick Medina come up prominently among a dozen newsmen and radio announcers. In a council resolution by Joseph E. Bulgo, Medina was congratulated for establishing an irresistible rapport with the people of Maui through his voice, diction and wit in sports broadcastings. In San Diego, Filipinos go for the *San Diego Union* mostly for the by-lined stories of Flores. Ayalin is a respected name in the editorial staff of the *Trumbull Times.* The efforts of Alex Esclamado *(Philippine News)*, Pedronio Ramos*(The Philippine Times)*, Teodoro Nolasco *(Philippine -American News)*, Cecilia F. Lopez *(Fil-American Express)*, J. T. Esteva *(Mabuhay Republic)* and M. H. Jacaban *(Bataan News)* are of course not to be minimized.

The Filipinos' contribution in business, though not startling, is as significant. A Filipino millionaire in Los Angeles, for instance, manufactures house doors and windows by the hundreds every day. Another Filipino millionaire provides the fish in Hawaii. Other front-rank Philippine businessmen in America are Larry Marquez, Tranquilino "Nonoy" Mendoza, the Heredias (Emil and Adelina), Soledad Alconcel, Emile Eisma, Manny David, Zosimo Majuelo, Jaime Licuanan, Manuel Canape, Solvador San Agustin, Ernesto Limcaco, Alfredo Tuazon, Frank Valdovino, Nelson Ayala, Ness Aquino, the Barons (Jose and Cecilia), Dr. Esteban Sadang, Eddie Olamit, Elena Desuyo, Teresita Villatuya, G. V. Manrobang and Jose Mandoriao.

G. Monty Manibog, Joe Agapay, Calvin Chao and Louis Garcia are making headway in law; Johnny Carandang, Pepito Ragasa, Ramon del Rosario in banking; Ramon Acuna-Felix, Silverio de la Vega, Tony Abagon, Cecilio Bulatao, Ernesto Tesoro, Olimpio S. Galon, Ted Dichirico, Ralph Duarte, Pete Lagusay, Dick Padrone and Lucho Singh in insurance; Butch Hermoso, Rod Estrada, Roy Morales, Remigio de Olazo and Ricardo Morada in government service; Gene Navarro and Larry Itliong in the labor front.

But more than in any other front, the Filipinos are best in the classroom. Whether in public or private schools, the youths seem to be there. They are A students or summa cum laude graduates. It is with them, in fact, that the promise of getting to the very top holds great expectations.

PART FOUR

THE LONG JOURNEY HOME

CHAPTER XVI

WHAT IS A FILIPINO IN AMERICA?

The Filipino in America is either a permanent resident or a naturalized American who finds no conflict nor inconsistency in being Filipino and American at the same time. He finds nothing unusual nor un-Filipino reciting the pledge of allegiance and singing the Star-Spangled Banner. Likewise, he finds nothing un-American genuflecting to things Philippines and proclaiming himself Filipino.

It is no case of self-identity amnesia nor conscious effort to delude himself. Contrary to what is often said of him, the Filipino knows himself quite well. He is at home with himself or with anyone. He can get by and in cases, go through. He can relate to any class of people or to almost any ethnic and racial group. He can speak at least three languages, plus five to ten Philippine dialects. He knows as much of U.S. history, geography, politics, the arts and sciences as the average American, having been brought up in the Old Country with a steady supply of *Time, Life, Look* and *Newsweek* magazines, and a supplementary fare of Hollywood movies, pop programs and TV commercials.

Visually, he is too brown to be either white or black, a condition very much to his favor. In the everyday confrontation between the Black and the White, he becomes the object of a tug-of-war.

But while avowedly brown, he is also consciously white, yellow, black and red. He is by marriage, adoption, religion, customs, education and living habits all races.

The white in him is understandably Spanish and American, with a sprinkling of English, Dutch, Portuguese and German; the yellow, Chinese and Japanese. Black is his old indigenous self. Dark-hued, kinky-haired and barely reaching five feet, he once was lord and master of the land, until the walnut-skinned Indonesians and Malays, coming in waves by sailboats from 800 B.C. to the 13th century, pushed him into the hinterlands.

The red in the Filipino is not something contrived. Though minimal to a degree, he is as Indian as a Mexican is Aztec. The Indian in him came all the way from Mexico when Spain, at one time, was forced to recruit Spaniards of the Mexican variety, to reinforce her strength in the Philippine archipelago. This resulted in the further co-mingling of races, and the coming into being of another crossbreed of Filipinos.

For schematic purposes, the Filipinos in America may be divided into six groups:

1. The first generation
2. The second generation
3. The veterans of World War II
4. Former civilian employees in American installations
5. Students and tourists managing to stay permanently
6. The new immigrants.

The first generation Filipinos are men in their fifties and sixties who have become juridically Americans. They have had their names streamlined. Juan Gloria has become Johnny Glory, Salvador Alicante Al Cante, Casimiro Boquinquicao (pronounced Ka-si-mi-ro Bo-king-ki-kao) Casmere Bouquet.

The Americanization of names, however, following citizenship eligibility in 1952, did not change matters overnight. The first generation Filipinos continued to seek each other's company and to speak their own tongue. They continued to regard the white man as their master, someone to say yes to and to flatter with servility at all times.

Now, whether their children, those born and bred in American soil, have caught up the last attitude is not certain. For today, the second generation Filipinos are for being different. They are for being at par with any, for asserting their status as Americans—as Filipino-Americans.

They do not look timid and docile. They are aggressive to the point of being blunt and brash. They are for competing in jobs, for proving excellence. They are for being righteous "and never mind if we are given up as hopeless radicals and a price tag is placed on our heads."

The war veterans—the third group of Filipinos in America—

on the other hand, are a bit more passive, having spent a good deal of their passion in war, and having, as it is, mellowed with age. They are for coasting along, for keeping their peace—their perspective rooted in the past, unchanged and unwavering. They are of the conviction that Bataan and Corregidor will always be there, that the ties of friendship between the Philippines and the United States will be special and lasting; and that, ultimately, the Philippines will forever be part of the American entity.

This sentiment is shared, understandably, by the fourth group of Filipinos, those who come from army depots and navy installations in Guam. They have, like the first generation Filipinos and the war veterans, sought naturalization without impingement of conscience. They have chosen to become Americans not so much for a change of heart as for expediency. To make things easy for them and their relatives.

The step has proved profitable. They found well-paying jobs. They got into better housing conditions, paving the way for the Philippine exodus.

Filipinos came as students, tourists and immigrants. They worked in hospitals and schools, the less qualified in gasoline stations, restaurants and factories. Before long there were more Pinoys of this kind than there were of the four other groups combined.

When the new Immigration Law came up in 1965, there were enough Filipinos in America to balance the ethnic proportion stipulated in the allocation. The Philippines was immediately good for 10,000 immigrants, looking up at the yearly ceiling allocation of 20,000.

In a collective sense, the Filipino in America is all this: immigrant-tourist-student-ex-depot employee-war veteran-American born and bred-and-oldtimer. He is also American. He finds himself a synthesis: workable, malleable and possible — a product of two worlds. He is Americon when it comes to will-power and energy. He is Filipino when it comes to temperament and sentiments. The American in him will make him want to do things by himself; the Filipino will make him want to help, and be helped, in the true spirit of *bayanihan.*

His sense of humor is both gay and sarcastic, frivolous and deadpan. His outlook more of the present and future than of the past. But for all the blending of the two worlds, the Filipino personality will always be predominant in him. Religion will play a big part in his life — dogmatically, ethically and ritually. He will make a lot of fuss on baptisms and confirmations, for the sake of *compadrazgo.*

He will be forgiving — but only to a point. He will not totally subscribe, for instance, to the pill, nor will he of the *padre* (Catholic priest) taking a wife. He will be tender and courtly to women, only if their morals are above board.

He will be flamboyant. Gregarious. Reckless. Expendable. Philosophic. Asked what or who a Filipino is in America, he is likely to come up with a classic answer, Ben Gurion-like: "A Filipino is anyone who feels and thinks he is — who says he is." It is a definition he does not just want to be smart about. It is something he has come to believe in, deeply and honestly.

CHAPTER XVII

SOME CONCLUSIONS

The Filipino who comes with expectations of seeing America in the manner he saw it in a dozen-or-so movies is in for some disappointments. For unless here on a fat allowance and only for a look-see, there will be no hundred-dollar shows for him, no eating out in first-class restaurants, nor doing over of big cities — not right away, anyway. He will be faced with the realities of looking around for a job that is up to his qualifications.

Five years ago, jobs were not a problem. The engineers among the Filipino immigrants found employment easily in Seattle; the doctors in the East; the nurses in hospitals, convalescent homes and public health; the other professionals in just about every respectable area of work. There were even second and third jobs for those bent on scuttling a fortune.

Today, the just arrived must have to depend on luck and grit if he is to avoid waiting on tables, driving taxicabs or running errands. He has to fall back on his resources. He can either start a business of his own, or, in the absence of a capital, make his skills pay-off. If he is that good, he will sell.

It would do well for him, though, to remember a few things. The *bahala na* attitude (come what may) or the *manana* habit (putting off things for the next day) must have to be overhauled. He must have to keep his appointments and not to apologize

continually for being one or two hours late.

He must not assume importance to give him cause to disparage others. (Says an American observer in this regard: "I have yet to meet a Filipino who has something nice to say about another Filipino, and this even about his closest friend. This kind of behavior throws me off.")

Inguitan, that spurious desire to see a countryman fall flat on his face, while a motivating factor, must have to be tempered, or pursued only in its positive aspects. Meaning, "the-first-Filipino-to-be-this-and-that" or "the-only-Filipino-to-hold-such-and-such-position" type of thing is to be encouraged, but not the activities of a fink.

He must have to cast aside his insularity, and the pettiness that seems to wrap his whole being. He must have to think of America in terms of an American, not a Filipino: he must not only expect to get but also to give.

He must have to do away with prejudices, and the isolation (if insulation) of his community. Involvement must go beyond ethnicity. It should not be "my people" but all people, not of Filipinos nor Americans but of all mankind.

Hired or self-employed, it would do well not to expect concessions, for none would be given him. He will have to stand on his own merits, and not on considerations of any kind. Making a fuss about being in the minority would only beg the issue and minimize the status of his race.

There are no shortcuts to   respect and recognition. He must have to compete, achieve and excel under conditions laid out for him.

The crux of the matter is either integration or assimilation. Webster's Dictionary defines assimilation as something "to make alike; to cause to resemble." Integration is the act of incorporating "diverse groups or individuals into a well-ordered community or society whose behavior is based on similar standards."

America is such a permissive place that loyalty to the fatherland (in this case a Filipino feeling and thinking more Filipino than Amercan) seems proper enough. But it is hoped that in the process he is made alike, "digested and melted down." That he uses less of his dialect and more of English, especially in a mixed crowd. That he stops talking about the Philippines being a better place to live in than America. That he gives up broiling "rotten" dried fish, or eating that smelly stuff of tiny shrimps, *bagoong*. That in the end he becomes like every American: assimilated.

Assimilation, however, is not his thing but integration. "The making up of a whole by adding together or combining the separate parts or elements; a making whole or entire." (Shorter Oxford Dictionary) He wants to add to, not detract from, the entire whole. To share his rich cultural heritage, to say nothing of such beautiful traits as respect for elders, closeness of family ties, loyalty to a benefactor, peculiar sense of humor, wit, his art and his trust in God.

Now, whether he can have his say on the matter is all up to him. The Filipinos in America today constitute a significant minority, small enough to watch, successful enough to take over important positions, and large enough to decide local election in certain places. The Filipino wanting to be heard cannot ask for a better chance.

APPENDICES

Appendix I

Filipino Organizations and Presidents in America 1970-1971

Abranan Club
Sandy Aragon
Ewa, Oahu, Hawoii

Abranian Club
Naty Velasco
San Francisco, California

Agoonians Association
of California
Federico Marinas
San Francisco, California

Aklan Association
Sancho Aclaro
Westwood, New Jersey

Aklan Association
Winston Acevedo
Monterey Park, California

Aklan Association Inc.
Ernesto Militar
San Francisco, California

Albuera-Leyte Association
Belen Engler
San Francisco, California

American Filipino Brotherhood
of Tacoma
Graciano Pingul Sr.
Tacoma, Washington

American Legion Post #603
Rodney Davies
Vallejo, California

American Legion Bataan Post
#600
Melanio Estopares
San Francisco, California

American Legion Rizal Post
#3698
George Balboa
Oakland, California

Anak Ti Batac Association
Jerry Bactat
Stockton, California

Annac Ti Batac
Cipriano Aquilizan
Pearl City, Oahu, Hawaii

Ang Filipina
Purita Latosa
Lodi, California

Annac Ti Caoayan
John Quiocho
Honolulu, Hawaii

A. R. Vibora Lodge #537 LDT
Godfrey LaMadrid
Seattle, Washington

Association of Filipino Americans
Sofronio Moreno
Hilo, Hawaii

Association of Philippine
Lawyers (USA)
Dionisio Aguila Marasigan
New York, New York

Association of Filipino Priests
Rev. Antonio Rances, J.C.D.
San Francisco, California

Aurora Lodge, LDT
Frances Mendoza
Salinas, California

Auxiliaries
Tito Sison
Vallejo, California

Baccarra Association
Cosme Bolosan
Waipahu, Oahu, Hawaii

Bachelor's Club
Fred Viloria
Chicago, Illinois

Badoc-Pinili Aid Association
Felipe Madarang
Honolulu, Hawaii

Bagumbayan Association
Nemesio Salazar
Chicago, Illinois

Balaan Catalina Society
Isidro Villaflor
Honolulu, Hawaii

Bataan-Corregidor Society
of America
Margaret Krsak-Koesen
San Francisco, California

Bataan-Corregidor Survivor's
Club
Rudolf Ramac
Seattle, Washington

Bataan Lodge, CDA
Carlos Malla
Seattle, Washington

Bataan Lodge #11, CDA
Gerry Serafino
San Francisco, California

Batangas Club of Chicago
Modesto Villa
Chicago, Illinois

Bauang Circle
Phillip Bautista
San Francisco, California

Bauangenian Club
Silvestre Tangalan
Seattle, Washington

Beautiful Love Council
#6254 KC
Jose J. Baron
Sacramento, California

Bicol Circle
Amancio Ergina
San Francisco, California

Bicolandia Association
Dr. Emmanuel Pangan
Brooklyn, New York

BIMAK
Rudyard Buyagawan
Los Angeles, California

Bohol Circle
Hugo Lafuente
San Francisco, California

Bohol Circle of Hawaii
Eugene Malalis
Honolulu, Hawaii

Bugallon Lodge #638
Ray Hipol
Seattle, Washington

Burgos Lodge #10 CDA
Ted Ranjo
Seattle, Washington

Cabadbaran Club
Joe Cravotto
Albany, California

Caballeros de Dimas-Alang
Pablo Parrocha
San Francisco, California

Caballeros de Dimas-Alang
Constancio Quinto
Pearl City, Oahu, Hawaii

Cagayan Valley Association
Don Alameda
San Francisco, California

Cagayano Circle
Amador Dominquez
Chicago, Illinois

Cardona Club
Jim Estrella
San Francisco, California

Catholic Filipino Guild
Julie Dumo
Chicago, Illinois

Cavite Association of California
Jose S. Aquino
South San Francisco, California

Cavite Association of San
  Diego
Felimon Adrid
San Diego, California

Cebu Brotherhood
Romy Madrigal
Harbor City, California

Cebu Circle
Sally B. Atkinson
San Francisco, California

Cebu Club
Susan Vitor
Chicago, Illinois

Circulo Pampangueno of
  California
Nick Benoza
San Francisco, California

Civic Associates
Nunelon Medallon
Honolulu, Hawaii

Claverianos Saranay Club of
  Hawaii
Pedro S. Tabangay
Waipahu, Oahu, Hawaii

Club Filipino
Jess Trompeta
Los Angeles, California

Contra Costa Association
Mel Diokno
Pittsburg, California

Corregidor Lodge #601 LDT
Senso Ramirez
Salinas, California

Corregidor Memorial Hall
Sixto Basconcillo
Honolulu, Hawaii

Dagohoy Lodge, LDT
Isidro Samforma
Stockton, California

Dagupan City Club
Denny Arcelona
Los Angeles, California

De la Salle Alumni Association
Dionisio Calvo
San Francisco, California

Del Pilar Lodge #629
A. C. Penor
Seattle, Washington

Democratic Club of New Jersey
Benny Francisco
Newark, New Jersey

Dimasalang Inc. of Sacramento
Max Ruiz
Sacramento, California

Diocesan Congress of Filipino
Catholic Clubs
Ambrosio Rivera
Honolulu, Hawaii

Dona Librada Lodge
Marie Brasil
Los Angeles, California

East-West Ladies Chapter
(Gran Oriente Filipino)
Cleothilde Mina
Puyallup, Washington

Epiphany Filipino Society
of San Francisco
Alberto Mitra
San Francisco, California

Evangelista Lodge #164 CDA
Alex Esclava
Seattle, Washington

Ewa Filipino Community
Association
Felix Clemente
Ewa, Oahu, Hawaii

Filipiniana Club
I. L. Villarubia
Los Angeles, California

Filipiniana Dance Troupe
Aurelia Viernes
Honolulu, Hawaii

Filipino Adult and Youth
Catholic Organization
Myrna Gunn
San Francisco, California

Filipino Alumni Association
Inc.
Antonio San Jose
Los Angeles, California

Filipino-American Armed
Forces Retired Association
Sid Vallador
San Francisco, California

Filipino-American Artist Guild
Madia-as D. Buenaflor
Los Angeles, California

Filipino American Association
of Portland
Silvestre Pulmano
Portland, Oregon

Filipino American Association
of St. Paul
Marcial Simpson
California

Filipino-American Catholic
Association
Amado Q. Cosio
Salinas, California

Filipino-American Catholic
Association
Dolores Pizzaro
Sacramento, California

Filipino-American Catholic
Club of Vallejo
Elizabeth Miguel
Vallejo, California

Filipino-American Citizens
League
Tony Ogilvie
Seattle, Washington

Filipino-American Civic
League
Fannie Hernandez
Salinas, California

Filipino-American Civic
League
Mrs. Tony Carpiso
Oakland, California

Filipino-American Community
Of Bremerton
Cris Pena
Port Orchard, Washington

Filipino-American Community
of Bremerton and Vicinity
Vincent Barrios
Bremerton, Washington

Filipino-American Community
of Castroville
Caridad Layus
Castroville, California

Filipino-American Community
of Monterey
Arsenio Turqueza
Monterey, California

Filipino-American Community
of Los Angeles
Dr. Dulzura Villaflor
Los Angeles, California

Filipino-American Community
of Northern & Central California
Mel Diokno
Pittsburg, California

Filipino-American Community
of Puget Sound
Johnny Mina
Puyallup, Washington

Filipino-American Community
of San Francisco
Necerita D. Revelo
San Francisco, California

Filipino-American Democratic
Club of New York
Tim Magistrado
Brooklyn, New York

Filipino-American Family Club
Nick Nicolas
San Francisco, California

Filipino-American Inter-Com-
munity Council
Ray Baldoz
Union Gap, Washington

Filipino-American Institute
Elizabeth Amores
San Francisco, California

Filipino-American Jaycees
Emil de Vera
Pinole, California

Filipino-American League
Vincent Costales
Port Lewis, Washington

Filipino-American Optimist
Club of Downtown Los
Angeles
Vic Zapanta
Los Angeles, California

Filipino-American Post #652
Santos M. Sabio
Salinas, California

Filipino-American Postal
Employees
Rufino Cacabelas
Seattle, Washington

Filipino-American Political
Association of California
Tranquilino Mendoza
Los Angeles, California

Filipino-American Political
Association (National)
Tranquilino Mendoza
Los Angeles, California

Filipino-American Political
 Association of Delano
Phillip Vera Cruz
Delano, California

Filipino-American Political
 Association of Fremont
Ubaldo Flores
Fremont, California

Filipino-American Political
 Association of Los Angeles
Benjamin Manibog
Los Angeles, California

Filipino-American Political
 Association of New York
Antonio Flores
New York, New York

Filipino-American Political
 Association of Oakland
Olivia Carpiso
Oakland, California

Filipino-American Political
 Association of Pismo Beach
Mrs. Apolinario Tablang
Pismo Beach, California

Filipino-American Political
 Association of San Diego
Cecilia Lopez
San Diego, California

Filipino-American Political
 Association of San Francisco
Anselmo Revelo
San Francisco, California

Filipino-American Political
 Association of Stockton
Martin Castillo
Stockton, California

Filipino-American Political
 Association of Vallejo
Ubaldo Flores
Vallejo, California

Filipino-American Political
 Association of San Fernando
Ralph Dapar
San Fernando, California

Filipino-American Political
 Association of West Los
 Angeles
Jess Trompeta
Los Angeles, California

Filipino-American Postal Em-
 ployees Association
Alfonso Aningalan
San Francisco, California

Filipino-American Professional
 Landscape Gardeners Ass'n
Cory Manangan
San Francisco, California

Filipino-American Retired U.S. Armed Forces Ass'n of Solano County
Ric Maravilla
Solano County, California

Filipino-American Society of California
Aida Escuton
San Francisco, California

Filipino-American South Market Neighborhood Association
Cielito Lucas
San Francisco, California

Filipino-American Teacher's Association of Washington
Encarnacion Tajon
Renton, Washington

Filipino-American Women's Club
Naty Carlyle
Seattle, Washington

Filipino-American Women's Club of Watsonville
Rosita Tabasa
Watsonville, California

Filipino-American Youth Organization
Agripino Edralin
Sacramento, California

Filipino Art Lover's Club
Rafaela Valentin
Honolulu, Hawaii

Filipino Bachelor's Society
Jose T. Dizon
San Francisco, California

Filipino Boy Scouts of California
Marcelino B. Lim
San Francisco, California

Filipino Brotherhood of California
Guillermo Mascardo
Fremont, California

Filipino Catholic Association
Ted Lapuz
Stockton, California

Filipino Catholic Association of San Francisco
Ted Sabiniano
San Francisco, California

Filipino Club
Maria Formalejo
San Francisco, California

Filipino Club of Arizona
Dr. Luis Tan
Phoenix, Arizona

Filipino Circle of Fremont
Mrs. Victor Ranoa
Fremont, California

Filipino Community of Alva-
rado
Ambrose Loyola
Alvarado, California

Filipino Community of Ancho-
rage, Alaska, Inc.
Claro Bermudez
Anchorage, Alaska

Filipino Community of Ante-
lope Valley
Marvin H. Wickham
California City, California

Filipino Community of Arvin
Elena Calaustro
Arvin, California

Filipino Community of Brooks
John Dundran
Brooks, Oregon

Filipino Community of Con-
cord
Apolinar Omania
Concord, California

Filipino Community of Dallas
Dallas, Texas

Filipino Community of Delano
Nash Basconcello
Delano, California

Filipino Community of East
Bay Area
Bernabe Flores
Berkeley, California

Filipino Community of Fair-
field
Cora Mock
Fairfield, California

Filipino Community of Fresno
William Gascon
Fresno, California

Filipino Community of Imperi-
al Valley
Tomas Rubio
Holtville, California

Filipino Community of Isleton
Ben Abulong
Isleton, California

Filipino Community of Kona
Severo Dimson
Kona, Hawaii

Filipino Community of Las
Vegas
Mel Salazar
Las Vegas, Nevada

Filipino Community of Los An-
geles
Milagros de la Cruz
San Pedro, California

Filipino Community of Mon-
terey Peninsula
Raymond Menes
Monterey, California

Filipino Community of Pitts-
burg
Apolio Eclips
Pittsburg, California

Filipino Community of Sacra-
mento
Leo Bautista
Sacramento, California

Filipino Community of Salinas
Valley
Manuel Luz
Salinas, California

Filipino Community of San
Diego
Ben Balanag
San Diego, California

Filipino Community of San
Francisco
Lorraine Wiles
San Francisco, California

Filipino Community of San
Luis Obispo
Ted Fermin
Arroyo Grande, California

Filipino Community of Santa
Barbara
Charles B. Versola
Santa Barbara, California

Filipino Community of Santa
Cruz
Johnny Isidro
Santa Cruz, California

Filipino Community of Seattle
Silvestre Tangalan
Seattle, Washington

Filipino Community of Solano
County
Feliciano Numar
Vallejo, California

Filipino Community of Stock-
ton and Vicinity
Johnny Latosa
Lodi, California

Filipino Community of Ventura
Coast
Rodolfo B. Salazar
Oxnard, California

Filipino Community of Wat-
sonville
Ben Ragsac
Watsonville, California

Filipino Community of Yuma
John Bermio
Yuma, Arizona

Filipino Cultural and Educa-
tional Society
Nono Navarro
Stockton, California

Filipino Dental Society of Cali-
fornia
Dr. Antonio Regadio
San Francisco, California

Filipino Executive Council
(N.J.)
Gerome V. Giron
Newark, New Jersey

Filipino Family Circle
Anne Sepe
Santa Maria, California

Filipino Family Fraternity
Ben Pena
California

Filipino Federation of America,
Inc.
Marion Rayray
Stockton, California

Filipino Immigrant National
Organization of Youth
Frank Bautista
San Francisco, California

Filipino Inter-Island Associa-
tion
Bernardine Batugo
Chatsworth, California

Filipino Nurses Association
Cecilia Ubengen
San Francisco, California

Filipino Nurses Association
of Seattle
Virginia Cacabelos
Seattle, Washington

Filipino Political Club of Hay-
ward
Frank Sacramento
Union City, California

Filipino Post #509, AL
Carmelito Llapitan
Chicago, Illinois

Filipino Professionals and Businessmen of San Francisco
Zoilo Inacay
San Francisco, California

Filipino Scholarship Foundation
Cora Manayan
Honolulu, Hawaii

Filipino Service Club of Fresno
Richard Campos
Fresno, California

Filipino Socio-Culturol Association
Vicente Ereneta
Whiting, Indiana

Filipino Social Club of New York
Ralph Langit
Brooklyn, New York

Filipino Society of St. Anthony
Leo Rentillo

Filipino Student Association
Polytechnic High School
Benita Sobremonte
San Francisco, California

Filipino Student Association
University of Washington
Ricardo Singson
Seattle, Washington

Filipino Teacher's Association
Virginia Santa Maria
San Francisco, California

Filipino Veterans of Foreign Wars
Nemesio Quillon
Long Island, New York

Filipino Women's Civic Organization
Annie Corpuz
Honolulu, Hawaii

Filipino Welfare Association Inc
Rosario Danao
Sacramento, California

Filipino Women's Club
Mrs. Bill Samson
Stockton, California

Filipino Women's Club
Julita Cruz
Chicago, Illinois

Filipino Women's Club of Bay Area
Mrs. Pete San Juan
Berkeley, California

Filipino Women's Club of Fresno
Pat Garcia
Fresno, California

Filipino Women's Club of Monterey
Mrs. Jack Figuerras
Monterey,, California

Filipino Women's Club of New York
Teresa Cacanindin
Springfield Garden, New Jersey

Filipino Women's Club of Salinas
Fanny Hernandez
Salinas, California

Filipino Women's Club of San Diego
Faye N. Ganaden
San Diego, California

Filipino Women's Club of San Francisco
Betty Gatchalian
San Francisco, California

Filipino Women's Club of Vallejo
Mrs. Nick Roldan
Vallejo, California

Filipino Women's Political League
Dr. Caro Manayan
Honolulu, Hawaii

Filipino Youth Activities of Seattle Inc.
Dorothy Cordova
Seattle, Washington

Forty Up Club
Jose Samdad
Honolulu, Hawaii

Garden State Filipino American Association
Saturnino Domingo
Jersey City, New Jersey

General Agueda Cahabagan #3
Rose Watt
Los Angeles, California

General Luna Lodge #8
Ben Arcelona
Los Angeles, California

General Tinio Lodge #67,
CDA
Gene Caponpon
Winalon, Washington

General Trias Lodge #21
Bennie Castillo
Los Angeles, California

Gran Oriente Filipino
Bruno Ramones
Salinas, California

Gran Oriente Filipino
Bataan Lodge
Carlos Malla
Seattle, Washington

Gran Oriente Filipino
Zamora Lodge
Severo Castillo
California

Gran Oriente Filipino
Severino Ruste
San Jose, California

Grand Council of Iloilo Circle
Inc.
Julie Velete
Stockton, California

Hawaii Council of Filipino
Catholic Clubs
George Ontiveros
Hilo, Hawaii

Hawaii Filipino Community
Council
Philip Onga
Hilo, Hawaii

Hawaii Filipinos of Waianae
Tony Mirafuentes
Waianae, Oahu, Hawaii

Hawaii Filipino Women's Club
Nancy Verano
Honolulu, Hawaii

Hermosa Dance Troupe
Rene Cortes
Chicago, Illinois

Hilo Sugar Filipino Club
Engracio Mondawe
Hilo, Hawaii

Honokaa Filipino Club
Emilio Pacyao
Honokaa, Hawaii

Ilocos Norte Aid Association
Justo de la Cruz
Waialua, Oahu, Hawaii

Ilocos Nortenian Association
Riano Santos
Woodridge, Illinois

Illocos Sur Association
Denny Acenan
San Francisco, California

Iloilo Circle
Ariston Armada
San Francisco, California

Iloilo Circle
Stockton, California

International Women's Club
Inc.
Conchita Lubrin
Sacramento, California

Junior Chamber of Commerce
East Bay
Pete San Juan
San Francisco, California

Kahirup International
Bernardo Buenaflor
Los Angeles, California

Kahuku Filipino Community
Ass'n.
Angel Ramos
Kahuku, Oahu, Hawaii

Kamuela Filipino Community
Ass'n.
Faustino Del Rosario
Kamuela, Hawaii

Karurukan-Dalisayan
Bataan No. 11
Santa Cruz, California

Kauai Council of Filipino
Catholic Clubs
Mercedes Fabro
Kauai, Hawaii

Kaunakakai Community As-
sociation
Eligio Ocampo
Kaunakakai, Molokai, Hawaii

Keaau Filipino Club
Maximo Gapol
Keaau, Hawaii

Kekaha Filipino Community
Victor Gapasen
Kekaha, Hawaii

Knights of Columbus
Sergio Acena
Seattle, Washington

Knights of Columbus (Colum-
bianas)
Rosalia Mendoza
Seattle, Washington

Knights of Columbus Council #6254
Jose Baron
San Francisco, California

Knights of Rizal
Jose Asuncion, Sec.
Irvington, New Jersey

Kohala Filipino Community Association
Mercedes Ver
Haui, Hawaii

Komokomo Filipino Community Ass'n
Melecio Esposo
Kealia, Kauai, Hawaii

Kurtistown Filipino Club
Eusebio Blas
Kurtistown, Hawaii

Kualapuu Filipino Community Ass'n
Igmidio Mina
Kualapuu, Hawaii

La Union Association
Sesinando Delmendo
Los Angeles, California

La Union Circle
Aquilino Corpuz
Alameda, Califirnia

La Union Circle
James Rillera
San Francisco, California

La Union Club
Frank Raguro
Evanston, Illinois

Ladies and Knights of Rizal
Necerita D. Revelo
San Francisco, California

Lanai Filipino Catholic Club
Johnny del Rosario
Lanai City, Hawaii

Lanai Filipino Community Ass'n
Lanai City, Hawaii

Laoag Saranay Club of Hawaii
Roque Pascual
Honolulu, Hawaii

Laoaguenian Association of Southern California
Lamberto Benito
Los Angeles, California

Loagueno Mutual Aid Ass'n
Mel Guillermo
San Francisco, California

Laoaguenians
Clemente Udasco
Castroville, California

Lapog Mother's Association
Mrs. Serafin Mutute
San Francisco, California

Lapulapu Lodge LDT
Bert Janoas
Stockton, California

Lebanon U.D. Gran Oriente
   Filipino
Mariano Arriola
Wapato, Washington

Legionaires del Trabajo
   In America Inc.
Roque de la Isla
Los Angeles, California

Legionaires del Trabajo
Antonio de los Santos
Stockton, California

Legionaires del Trabajo
Ancheta Mauricio
Vallejo, California

Leonor Rivera Lodge #56
Cecilia Dimaya
San Francisco, California

Leyte Association of Northern
   California
Elizabeth Apostol
San Francisco, California

Ligaya Lodge, CDA
Joan Abenojar
San Francisco, California

Livermore Filipino Community
   Sp. Immigrant Alliance
Carlos R. Santos
San Francisco, California

Los Angeles Philippine Junior
   Women's Club
Suzanne Iremedio
Los Angeles, California

Los Angeles Philippine Wom-
   en's Club
Mrs. Teofilo Alemania
Los Angeles, California

Luvimi Club
Joe Barlon
Ewa, Oahu, Hawaii

Luzonian Aid Association
Clemente Duclayan
Honolulu, Hawaii

Luz-Vi-Minda Club
Nilo Quintilla
Seattle, Washington

Mabuhay Golf Association
Ramon Barretto
San Francisco, California

Magellan Post #604, AL
Mercelino Ignacio
Broderick, California

Maharlikan Club
Francisco Latorre
Hilo, Hawaii

Mangaldan Associaton
Leonardo Soriano
San Francisco, California

Manila Post #465 AL
Numeriano Lagmay
Los Angeles, California

Manuel Roxas Post #798
Lucio Rabe
Stockton, California

Maria Clara Lodge
Paula Daclan
Stockton, California

Maria Clara Lodge #132
Macaria Martin
Seattle, Washington

Marina Dizon Lodge #381
CDA
Aida Escuton
San Francisco, California

Masantolenos of California
San Francisco, California

Maui Council of Filipino
  Catholic Clubs
Domingo Barbosa
Kahalui, Hawaii

Maui Filipino Community
  Council
Paul Pladera
Wailuku, Hawaii

Maunaloa Filipino Community
  Association
Ireneo Vergara
Maunaloa, Molokai, Hawaii

Maynila Lodge #17, CDA
Adelia G. Casas
Salinas, California

Molokai Filipino Catholic Club
Maile Pidot
Maunaloa, Molokai, Hawaii

Molokai Filipino Community
  Council
Antonio Abrahano
Kualapuu, Molokai, Hawaii

Moncado Foundation Inc.
Juan Acel
Capt. Cook, Hawaii

Moncado Foundation Inc.
Mario Moncado
Honolulu, Hawaii

Morong Club, The
  Andres Evangelista
San Francisco, California

Mutya Ng Silangan Dance
  Troupe
Helen Marte Bautista
San Francisco, California

Narvacan Association
Pete Cabarloc
Los Angeles, California

Native Sons and Daughters of
  Dingras
Antonio Torres
San Francisco, California

Native Sons of Lapog
Fred Guerrero
San Francisco, California

Naalehu Filipino Community
  Ass'n
Naalehu, Hawaii

Nortenian League
Joe Pepito Ignacio
Seattle, Washington

Northenians San Francisco-Bay
  Area
Sydney Suguitan
San Francisco, California

Nueva Vizcaya Association
Donald O'Connel
Chicago, Illinois

Nueva Vizcaya Organization
Jack Liban
Colma, California

Nueva Vizcaya Organization
  of California
Vic Hermoso
San Francisco, California

Numancia Aid Association
Dr. Ernesto Mabalon
Stockton, California

Oahu Council of Filipino
  Catholic Clubs
Josephine Pablo
Honolulu, Hawaii

Oahu Filipino Community
    Council
Pol Ragasa
Waipahu, Oahu, Hawaii

Occidental Negros Provincial
    Hospital Alumni Association
Zeralda Dacanay
Evanston, Illinois

Olekele Filipino Community
    Ass'n
Alipio Alvarado
Kaumakani, Kauai, Hawaii

Optimist Club of Richmond
Benjamin San Agustin
San Francisco, California

Paauhau Filipino American
    Club
Melecio Lacuesta
Paauhau, Hawaii

Paauilo Filipino Community
Elias Domingo
Paauilo, Hawaii

PACE
Ron Quidachay
San Francisco, California

Pahala Filipino Community
Pahala, Hawaii

Pahoa Filipino Community
    Ass'n
Remigio Salazar
Pahoa, Hawaii

Pampanga Circle of Hawaii
Ray Ocampo
Pearl Harbor, Hawaii

Pangasinan Association of
    Seattle
Felix Cornelio Mislang
Seattle, Washington

Pangasinan Association of Long
    Beach
Aurelia de la Vega
Carson, California

Pangasinan Association of
    Sacramento
Leo Bautista
Sacramento, California

Pangasinan Association of
    Salinas
Cornelio Supnet
Salinas, California

Pangasinan Association of
    Vallejo
Ceferina Dulay
Vallejo, California

Pangasinan Club of Hawaii
Martin Menor
Waialua, Oahu, Hawaii

Paoay-Currimao Hawaii Ass'n
Gregorio Guerrero
Honolulu, Hawaii

Papaikou Filipino Community
Ass'n
William Atis
Papaikou, Hawaii

Pearl of the Orient Club
Mary Ganotise
San Francisco, California

Pearl of the Orient Troupe
Orlando Valentin
Honolulu, Hawaii

Pepeekeo Filipino Community
Ass'n
Artemio Sensano
Pepeekeo, Hawaii

Perlas del Oriente
Lizatio Ortilla
Vallejo, California

Philippine American Art
Foundation
Estrella Salaver
San Francisco, California

Philippine American Bowling
League
Paul Clavecilla
Chicago, Illinois

Philippine American Catholic
Club of Watsonville
Nina Almihiana
Watsonville, California

Philippine American Cultural
Society
Mike Magdaluyo
San Francisco, California

Philippine American Friend-
ship Club
Pastor Amiscua
Seattle, Washington

Philippine American Institute
of California
Sid Vallador
San Francisco, California

Philippine American Society of
Santa Clara
Norberto Ricamora
San Jose, California

Philippine American Voter's
League
Marcos Mata
Los Angeles, California

Philippine Association of University Women
Shirley Dimapilis
San Francisco, California

Philippine Club of Lincoln University
Guillermo Rufino
San Francisco, California

Philippine Club of the University of San Francisco
Harris Sodon
San Francisco, California

Philippine Communities Executive Council
Precioso Nicanor
Long Island, New York

Philippine Cultural Foundation of Hawaii Inc.
Soledad Alconcel
Honolulu, Hawaii

Philippine Dental Association of Los Angeles
Dr. Jose Umali
Los Angeles, California

Philippine Cultural Society
Gloria Toralballa
Englewood, New Jersey

Philippine Medical Association in America
Dr. Renato Berroya
New York, New York

Philippine Medical Association of Chicago
Dr. Adolfo Maglaya
Chicago, Illinois

Philippine Medical Association of New York - New Jersey
Dr. Carmen Estacion
New York, New York

Philippine-New York Jaycees
Bobby Esperancilla
Brooklyn, New York

Philippine Nurses Association
Carmen Decolongan
Chicago, Illinois

Philippine Nurses Association
Mrs. A. M. Cardenas
New York, New York

Philippine Nurses Club
Delia Goggins
Los Angeles, California

Philippine Post #1164 AL
Charles Goldstein
California

Philippine Scouts Association
of America
Capt. Leonard Cancio
Marina, California

Philippine Society
Jess Esteva
San Francisco, California

Philippine Technical and Professional Society
Rizal Pahati

Philippine Technical Society
Carlos Manalo
Chicago, Illinois

Philippine War Brides Ass'n
Julie Nonog
Seattle, Washington

Piddig Ilocos Norte Association
Marcos Valledor
Berkeley, California

Piddiguenos of Antioch
Segundo Cudiamat
Antioch, California

Piddiguenos of Hawaii
Pio Lacuesta
Honolulu, Hawaii

Progessive Youth of Morong
in America Inc.
Andy Evangelista
Daly City, California

Puna Filipino American Club
Vicente Arkangel
Olaa, Hawaii

Puna Filipino Community Ass'n
Frank Latorre
Keaau, Hawaii

Quezon Lodge, LDT
Frank Gampornia
Soledad, California

Quezonian Association of
Chicago
Vicente M. Correa
Chicago, Illinois

Ramon Magsaysay Lodge,
CDA
Frank Velasco
Wapato, Washington

Region #7, LTD
Roman Quino
Salinas, California

Rigidor Lodge #5, CDA
Jerry Bactat
Stockton, California

Rizal Lodge #3, CDA
Leonardo Cancio
Marina, California

Sampaguita Women's Circle
Dolly R. Antony
Torrance, California

Samar-Leyte Association
Salud Albarico
Los Angeles, California

Samarenos of California
Pete Zamboanga
Albany, California

San Nicolas Pangasinan
    Brotherhood Association
Gene del Rosario
Seattle, Washington

San Nicolasenos of Hawaii
Antone C. Cacatian
Honolulu, Hawaii

San Vicente Ferrer Club
Eutiquio Lontayo
Ewa, Oahu, Hawaii

San Vicent Ferrer Club
Jose Josol
Honolulu, Hawaii

Santa Catalina Association
Johnny Rabaca
Stockton, California

Santa Maria Association
Leon V. Acosta
Los Angeles, California

Santo Nino Brotherhood
Teodorico Nacion
Kaneoke, Hawaii

Saturnina Lodge #5 CDA
Carmen Cancio
Marina, California

Seattle Post #6599, Veterans
    of Foreign Wars
Nemesio Domingo
Seattle, Washington

Seattle Post #6599 VWF
    Ladies Auxiliary
Adelina Domingo
Seattle, Washington

Siquijor Association
Pacifico Bantilan
Stockton, California

Siquijor Association
Jacinto Clavo
Thornton, Califirnia

Siquijornon Club
Pastor Limatoc
Waipahu, Oahu, Hawaii

Shangrila-Filipina Inc.
Paloma Osmena
New York, New York

Sierra Madre Lodge, LDT
Sally Guieb
Salinas, California

Sinaitenians of California
Marcelino Ines Jr.
Torrance, California

Sofia de Vera Lodge, CDA
Felicidad Ramirez
Lathrop, California

Solsona Association if Hawaii
Manuel Guillermo
Hawaii

Sons and Daughters of Bin-
maley
Arcade Terrado
Concord, California

Sons and Daughters of
Cabugao Ilocos Sur
Paul Serna
Berkeley, California

Sons and Daughters of Ilocos
Region
Cirilo Sinfuego
Puunene, Maui, Hawaii

Sons and Daughters of Santa
Maria
Seattle, Washington

Sons of Macabebe
Frank Mendoza
Daly City, California

Sons of Narvacan
Fernando Cabacang
Salinas, California

Sons of Paoay
Ben Bagasao
Los Angeles, California

Tagalog Civic Club
Chito Camonayan
Honolulu, Hawaii

Talisay Association
Celestino Labuga
Stockton, California

Tanay Club of America
Felix Leonidas
Oakland, California

Tandang Sora Lodge #46
Mrs. Quintin Valenzuela
Los Angeles, California

Tarlac Club of Los Angeles
Jose de Leon
Los Angeles, California

Tarlakenians, The
Alfonso Castillo
Salinas, California

Teodora Alonzo Lodge, LDT
Concepcion Lagura
Stockton, California

Three Stars Lodge
Mary Hullana
Vallejo, California

Tilapas Lodge, LDT
Bonnie Cayetano
Salinas, California

Timaraw Club
Diosdado C. Avecilla
Honolulu, Hawaii

Torona Lodge #65
Florentino Catimon
Pasadena, California

Trinity County Filipino
   Community
Mrs. Dee Lizardo
Thornton, California

Tyre Lodge, Free & Accepted
   Masons
Joseph P. Mendoza
Seattle, Washington

Unified Filipino-American
   Service Organization
Alex Andres
Wilmington, California

United Bacarrinios of America
Ted Passion
San Francisco, California

United Filipino Association
Ness Aquino
San Francisco, California

United Filipino American
   Association
Florentino Gan
Imperial Beach, California

United Filipino Council of
   Hawaii
Dr. Mario P. Bautista
Honolulu, Hawaii

United Filipinos of Kona Club
Andres Macatiag
Capt. Cook, Kona, Hawaii

United Pangasinanes Association of America
Joseph Soy
San Francisco, California

United Vintarians of USA
Max Leano
San Francisco, California

University of Washington
Filipino Alumni Association
Manuel Rustia
Seattle, Washington

Varona Lodge, CDA
A. Torda
Stockton, California

Varona Village Social Club
Martin Calamaan
Ewa, Hawaii

Villasinian Rising Sun Association
Bob Uminga
Salinas, California

Visayan Circle
Antonio Boromeo
Seattle, Washington

Waialua Filipino Community Ass'n
Andres Lacuesta
Waialua, Oahu, Hawaii

Waimanalo Filipino Community Ass'n
Rufino Burgonio
Waimanalo, Oahu, Hawaii

Waimanalo Saranay Club
Quirino Olegario
Waimanalo, Oahu, Hawaii

Waimea Filipino Club
Jack Ignacio
Kamuela, Hawaii

Waipahu Filipino Cimmunity Ass'n
Pedring Tampon
Waipahu, Oahu, Hawaii

Whitmore Filipino Community Ass'n
Pascual Bautista
Whitmore, Wahiawa, Hawaii

Women's Auxiliary Bataan Post #600
Maria Estorpe
San Francisco, California

Women's Auxiliary Manuel
   Roxas Post #798
Mrs. Fred Yurong
Stockton, California

Women's Catholic Association
   of Pittsburg
Candida Ripalda
Pittsburg, California

Appendix II

THE PHILIPPINE SUMMER SCHOOL*

The idea first came up with the Philippine community in Los Angeles. Why not a cultural school for children of Filipino-American parentage? That way the children will be kept busy in summer and out of any mischief. More importantly, the children will be able to pick up a number of things which they will not elsewhere. They will be able to get acquainted with their parents' way of life. A school such as this will give them the opportunity of making friends with children of other Filipinos in the locale.

---

* *This is the accompanying piece (written by the author) for the Summer School Project which won an International award in 1970 for the Evening Optimists of Downtown Los Angeles, in a competition sponsored by the International Optimists.*

Having these for immediate goals, the elders in the Philippine community immediately · went to work. Funds were raised, teachers screened and parents notified. The response was heart-warming. Children within the neighborhood of 50 miles were brought in, reluctantly at first, for lessons in Philippine history, geography, native songs and Pilipino.

It was an auspicious start. What the community lacked in know-how the members more than made up in enthusiasm. In a week's time the children were clamoring to be brought to school everyday, instead of just being led to it every other day. They learned to commit to memory dates in Philippine history, to speak conversational Pilipino. They even managed to pronounce names properly, from Jo-see Ray-chel to Jose Rizal, Man-u-el Kwi-son to Manuel Quezon. Soon they were telling their parents things about the old country, like the salambao (fish net held aloft by a long pole) or about the narra and the Sampaguita, national tree and flower of the land, respectively. In no time they were able to carry such tunes as *Chit-chirit-chit, Dandansoy, Bahay Kubo, Leron-leron-sinta,* or the more difficult ones like *Walay Angay, Mutya ng Pasig* and *Sapagkat Ikaw ay Akin.*

This went on for two wonderful summers. But for some reasons interest wore out on the part of the original organizers. And for one year, there was no summer school, no singing and dancing. No little boys and girls trying to speak a quaint language.

Everyone started to look around — to ask questions. This was the time the Evening Optimists of Downtown Los Angeles came into the scene. They saw something laudable in the project. The school brought the children together; it gave them the chance to imbibe their own culture. But more than that, the school served as a springboard towards their search for identity.

Optimist Zosimo D. Majuelo, then head of the group, sent out circulars to this effect. Actually, there was very little need for a ballyhoo. The idea was long since bought — sold. All that was needed really was a reminder — and that was what Majuelo's circular did. Immediately, there was a rush of enrollees on all levels. A place to house the children then became a problem, but not for long.

The Filipino Christian Church in Union Avenue offered its facilities. A working budget was easily raised as cash poured in from all quarters, notably the Philippine Consulate in Los Angeles, the Sampaguita Women's Circle, the L. A. Junior Philippine Women's Club, Leyte-Samar Association, Philippine Technical and Professional Society, Inc., Manila's ABS Television, the Filipino Community, Philippine Airlines, Phil-Am Travel Agency, Pasay and Nipa Hut restaurants and from individual sources.

Towards August, after eight weeks of school grind, there were definite signs of accomplishment in the realm of knowledge and manners. Children were using the particle *po* after every statement when talking to elders. They were conversant with Limahong, the river pirate; with Buddha, canonized as saint. They learned the difference between maguey and rattan. The boys learned the rudiments of basket weaving, the girls embroidery.

But school was not all book learning and catching up on a native trade. It was also going to a picnic and being in the company of elders. It was taking pointers on diving, swimming and bowling, from a dozen athletically-minded members of the Club. In a sense it was an opportunity for the young to be with mature adults and vice-versa.

Commencement day saw youngsters misty-eyed, wondering whether there was going to be another summer school. "Certainly," says Summer School Director Roy Morales. "There will be a cultural school next year and in the years to come. Next year though, there will be classes for adults. The adults feel that they deserve a share of what the school has to offer by way of academics, social consciousness and extra curricular activities."

There is even talk of holding classes on a 10-month basis, instead of just eight weeks every summer. The demand has become that great.

INDEX

NOTE

The name Filipinos was used to refer to all persons of Philippine stock, whether just arrived or three generations back. Having to mention Filipino-Americans repeatedly would have proved awkward and tedious.

ALFREDO N. MUNOZ put in three years of work to complete this book, in-between heading a market study for a leading newspaper and magazine. Born in Libon, Albay, the Republic of the Philippines, he taught college English and literature for over twenty years, wrote short stories and articles, conducted a column for a weekly women's magazine, in addition to editing a literary-movie magazine in Manila. His first book on outstanding Filipinos, published in 1968, will be updated to include Filipinos in the United States.